TABLE OF CONTENTS

Introduction v

Subjects/Predicates/Articles 1

Direct Objects 7

Adjectives 14

Subjective Complements 22

Verb Phrases 30

Adverbs (Time, Place, and Manner) 33

Compound Predicates 41

Compound Subjects 49

Compound Direct Objects 58

Imperatives 67

REVIEW: Direct Objects 69

REVIEW: Adjectives 71

REVIEW: Subjective Complements 73

REVIEW: Adverbs (Time, Place, and Manner) 75

REVIEW: Compound Predicates 77

REVIEW: Compound Subjects 79

REVIEW: Compound Direct Objects 81

Answer Key 83

Diagramming Sentences

for Young Catholics

LEVEL 1 WORKBOOK

By Sean O'Connor

© 2022 Seton Press
All rights reserved.
Printed in the United States of America

Seton Press
1350 Progress Drive
Front Royal, VA 22630
Phone: (540) 636-9990

For more information, visit us on the web at www.setonpress.com.
Contact us by e-mail at info@setonpress.com.

INTRODUCTION

What is sentence diagramming?

Sentence diagramming is a visual representation of the structure of a sentence.

What is the point of learning sentence diagramming?

Some parents and students see the process of labeling words and placing a sentence into a diagram as a pointless exercise. However, learning how to diagram a sentence has three main benefits:

1. It allows kinesthetic and visual learners to grasp and understand English grammar since they are able to physically draw and see grammatical functions in the sentence;

2. It encourages and prompts students to think and analyze the language, increasing right-brain activity. This increased analytical focus is an easy way for students to learn and understand both the syntax and underlying structural relationships of the English language. Once they have a solid understanding of the structures, students are better equipped to see the parallels and differences between English and other languages, ultimately making a second or third language easier to learn.

3. With its analytical focus, sentence diagramming can also improve the ability of students to express themselves clearly and logically. Being able to communicate ideas effectively in writing is a valuable skill in any profession or state-in-life. Diagramming a sentence into its component parts enables the student to determine the best way to revise and improve the expression of their ideas.

What can I expect from this book?

Level 1 introduces students to diagramming using familiar and simple sentence structures they can recognize. They will start with subject-predicate sentences and conclude with imperative sentences. *Level 2* will proceed from that point and progress to more complex sentence structures.

How do I use this book?

If your student needs furthur practice in sentence diagramming or grammar, this workbook will help meet that need. It is important to note that the descriptions of the various parts of speech and grammar are not dicussed at length in this workbook. The function of the workbook is to augment a student's early study of English grammar and sentence diagramming.

For each section, there are four exercises and a review section in the back. Since this is a beginner-level workbook on sentence diagramming, the student is given pre-arranged sentence diagrams.

Being a consumable workbook, students are encouaged to write directly in the workbook so they can focus more on identifying and placing the various parts of speech in the correct places than drawing the actual diagrams.

Finally, an answer key is provided with this workbook which allows students to check their work.

Exercise 1
Students are given a list of sentences and are asked to underline or circle certain words or phrases. After marking them, students will diagram the sentences.

Exercise 2
Students are asked to create their own sentences to fill the given diagrams. Learning how to form sentences to fit a certain diagram allows students to practice their understanding of the various parts of speech with their own sentences.

NOTE: The answer key does not provide answers for this exercise due to the variety of sentences students may create.

Exercise 3
Students are given scrambled sentences and will arrange the sentences in the correct order and then diagram them. This exercise helps students to see each part of a sentence as a unit of language (subjects, predicates, direct objects, etc.)

Exercise 4
Students are given pre-diagrammed sentences and are asked to identify the errors and then diagram the sentences correctly.

Review
The review section contains additional exercises for students to practice their diagramming. Since diagramming skills are cumulative, it is also a useful tool for assessing a student's retention of previous concepts.

NOTE:
 Subject/Predicate/Articles, Verb Phrases, and Imperatives are simpler concepts and are not given review sections.

Name _____

DIAGRAMMING Level 1

SUBJECTS/PREDICATES/ARTICLES

The **subject** and **predicate** are the basic building blocks of the sentence. First, find the verb that expresses action (What is happening? such as *run, sleep*) or being (What is or feels? such as *am, was*). The verb functions as the **predicate** of the sentence.

Next, find the **subject**. The classic way to find the **subject** is to ask: *Who/What* is doing the action or being? Usually, a noun or pronoun functions as the **subject** of the sentence.

Finally, **articles**, which also are called **limiting adjectives**, can be found before a noun and are either definite (the) or indefinite (a, an) articles.

To diagram a **simple sentence** (only a **subject** and a **predicate**), start by drawing a horizontal line bisected by a vertical line which separates the **subject** from the **predicate**. **Articles** or **limiting adjectives** are placed on diagonal lines underneath the noun(s) they modify.

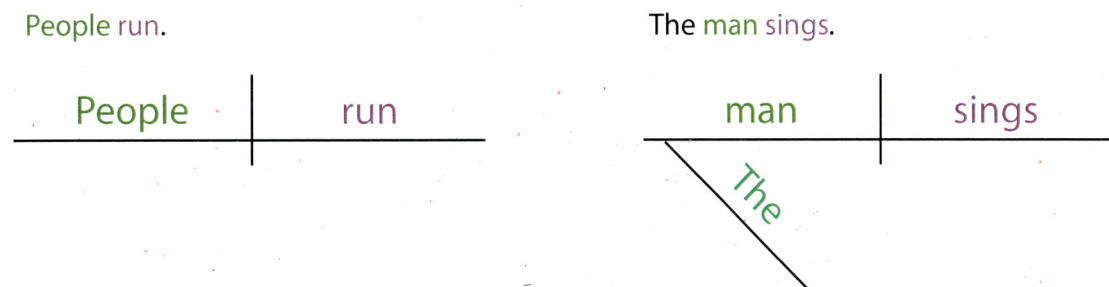

Exercise 1

In each of the following sentences, circle the subject and underline the predicate. Then diagram each sentence.

1. Cats jump.

2. The truck starts.

Subjects/Predicates/Articles 1

DIAGRAMMING Level 1

3. Dogs bark.

4. The boy yelled.

5. Sharks swim.

6. The leaves fell.

7. A bird dives.

8. Girls laugh.

Name

DIAGRAMMING Level 1

9. Airplanes fly.

10. A mouse scurried.

Exercise 2

Create sentences with a subject and a predicate to fit these diagrams. Then write each one on the correct diagram.

1.

2.

3.

Subjects/Predicates/Articles 3

DIAGRAMMING Level 1

4.
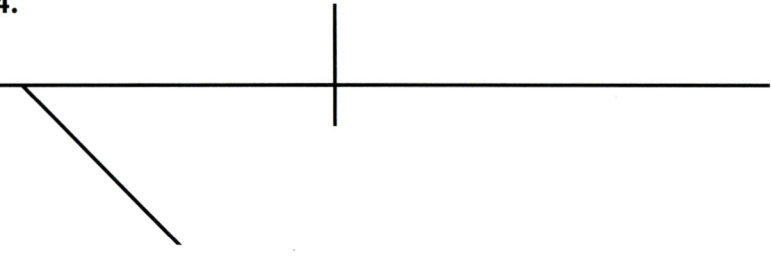

5.
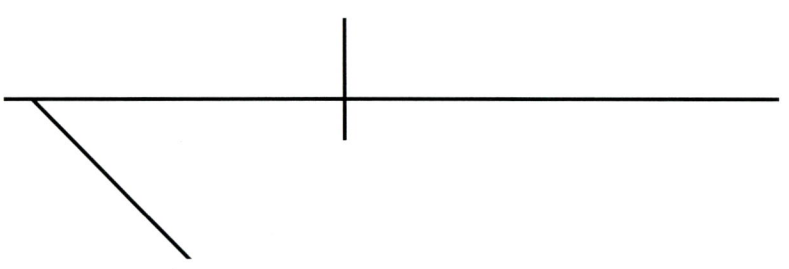

Exercise 3

Unscramble the groups of words to make complete sentences. Write the sentences on the blank lines. Then diagram them.

1. baked baker the _____

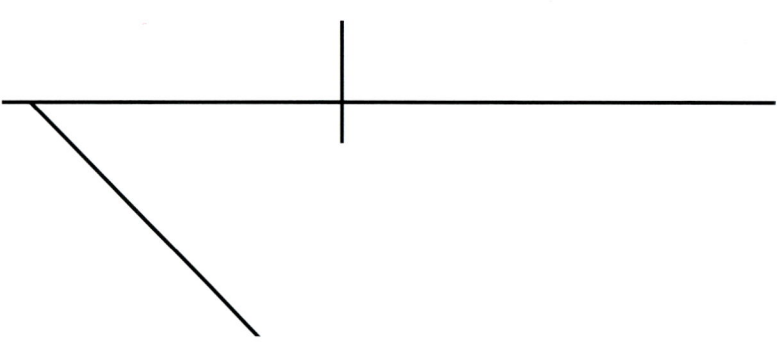

2. believes he _____

4 Subjects/Predicates/Articles

Name

DIAGRAMMING Level 1

3. artist an creates _____

4. dance ballerinas _____

5. the writes student _____

Exercise 4

Find the mistakes in the following diagrams. Then, diagram the sentences correctly on the given, blank diagrams. Note: you may need to fix the diagram by drawing a new line(s).

1. The hat fell.

DIAGRAMMING Level 1

2. The man studied.

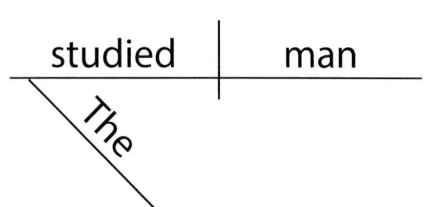

3. Bees sting.

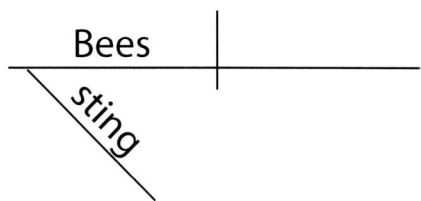

4. A child hides.

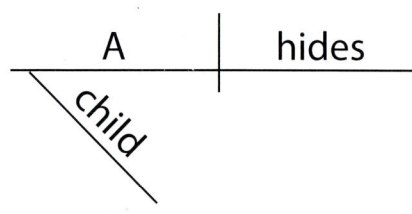
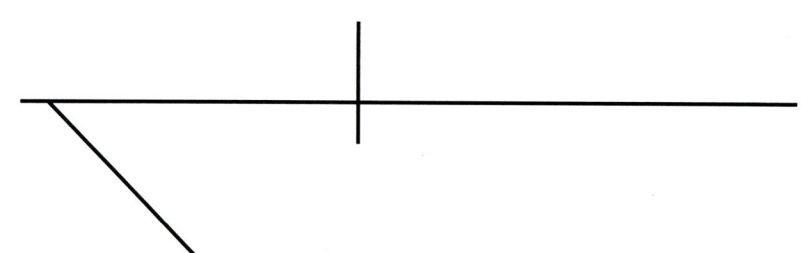

5. The phone rang.

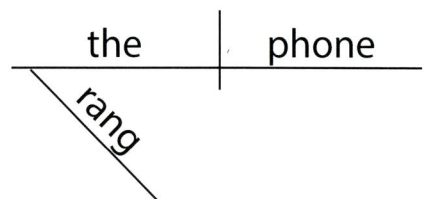
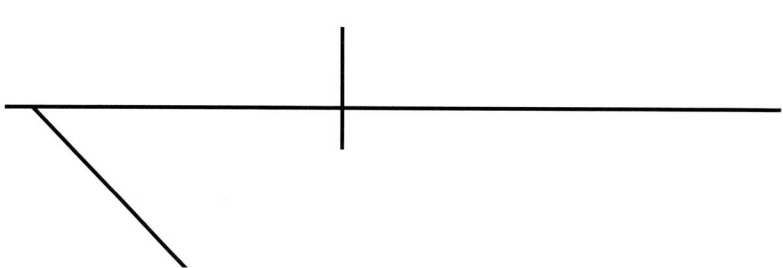

Name

DIAGRAMMING Level 1

DIRECT OBJECTS

In a sentence, the **direct object** receives the action of the **predicate**. The direct object answers the question *whom?* or *what?* after the action word.

To diagram a **direct object**, draw a short vertical line *which does not cross the horizontal line* after the **predicate**. Place the **direct object** after the short vertical line and any **articles** that modify the direct object on a slanted line underneath it.

The mother packed a **bag**.

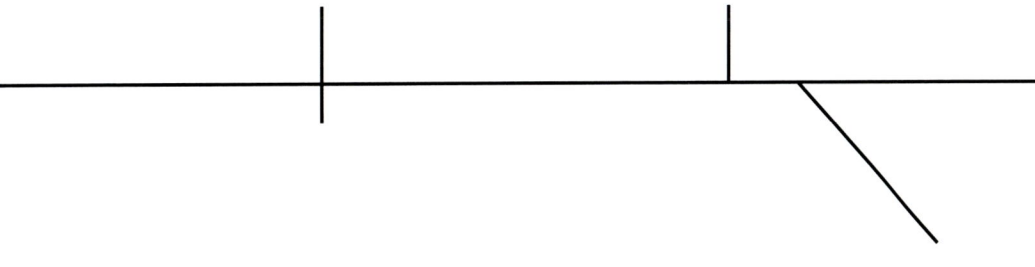

David threw the **ball**.

Exercise 1

In each of the following sentences, circle the subject, underline the predicate once and the direct object twice. Then diagram each sentence.

1. She read the newspaper.

2. Juan wrote letters.

Direct Objects 7

DIAGRAMMING Level 1

3. The wind rips the sails.

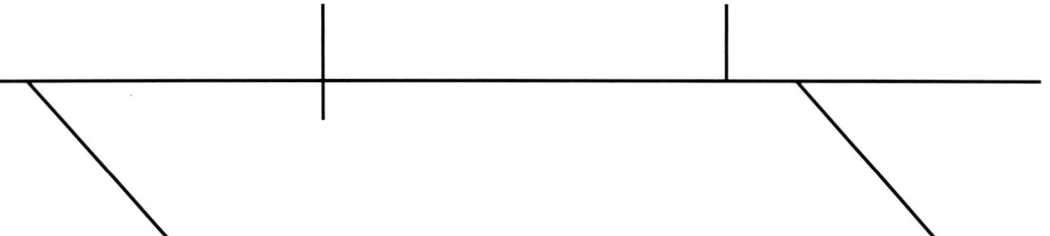

4. God saved her.

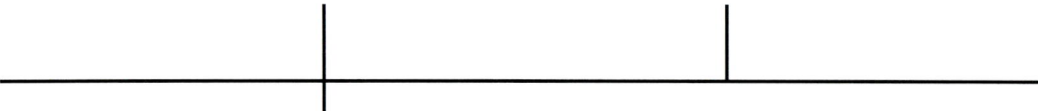

5. Fire burns wood.

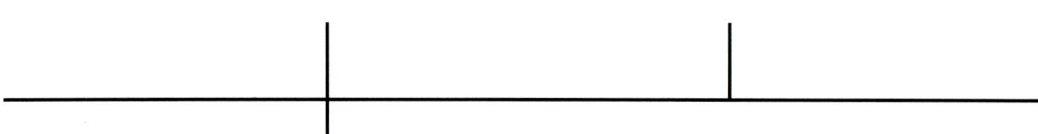

6. Margaret splashed Mark.

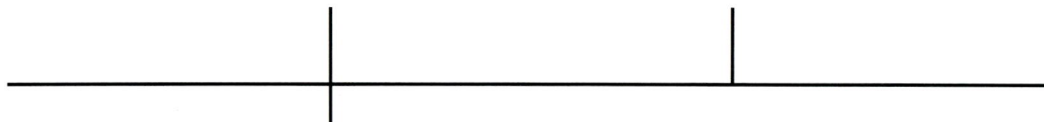

7. A jogger found the dog.

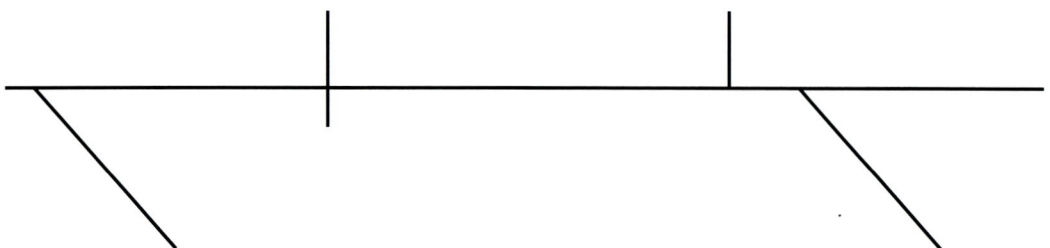

DIAGRAMMING Level 1

Name

8. Henry told a joke.

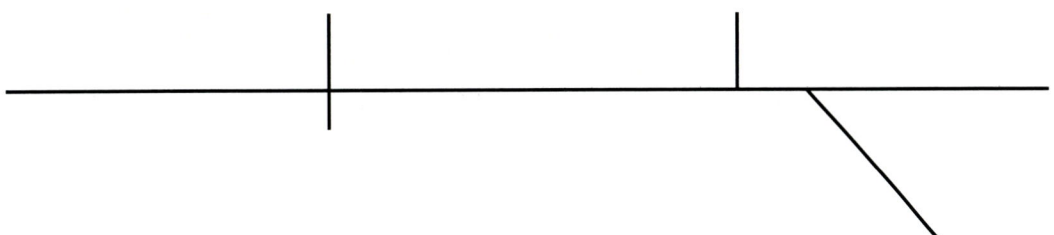

9. Jerome cleaned the room.

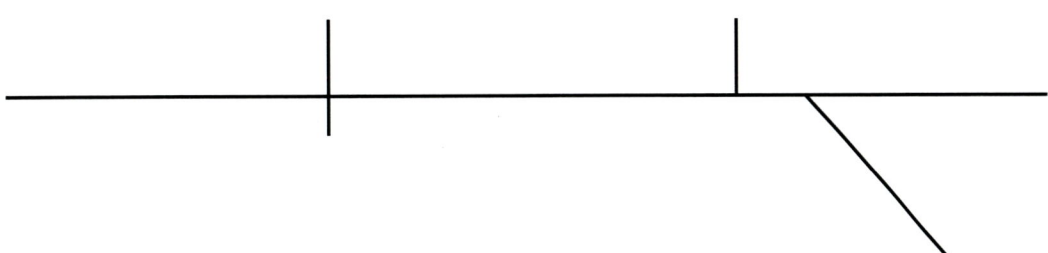

10. The shark ate the fish.

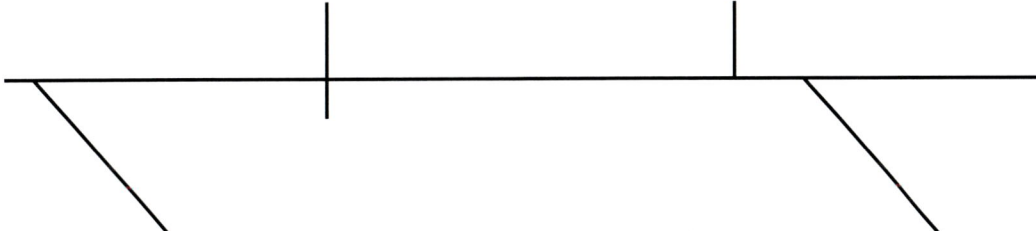

Direct Objects **9**

DIAGRAMMING Level 1

Exercise 2

Create sentences with a direct object to fit these diagrams. Then write each one on the correct diagram.

1.

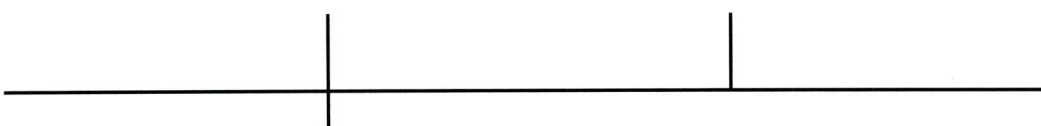

2.

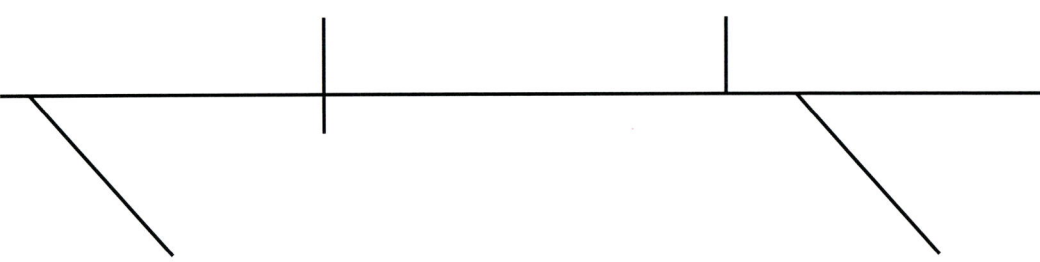

3.

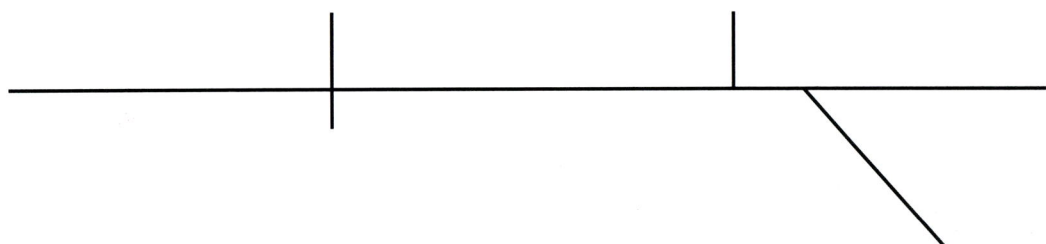

4.

Name

DIAGRAMMING Level 1

5.

Exercise 3

Unscramble the groups of words to make complete sentences. Write the sentences on the blank lines. Then diagram them.

1. pies bakes Norman _____

2. found him Elizabeth _____

3. the chewed dog bone the _____

Direct Objects 11

DIAGRAMMING Level 1

4. books read students

5. I question the answered

Exercise 4

Find the mistakes in the following diagrams. Then, diagram the sentences correctly on the given, blank diagrams. Note: you may need to fix the diagram by drawing a new line(s).

1. Tristan played a violin.

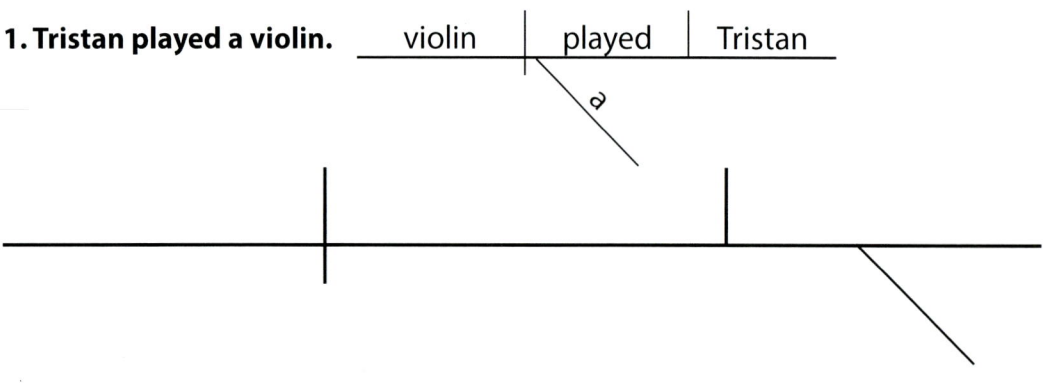

2. Priests celebrate Mass.

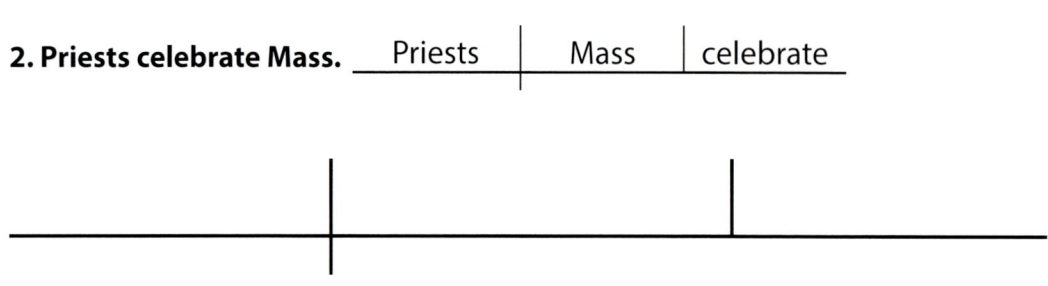

12   Direct Objects

Name

DIAGRAMMING Level 1

3. The paddle slapped the water.

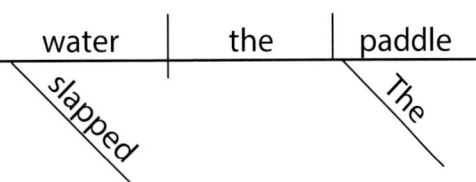

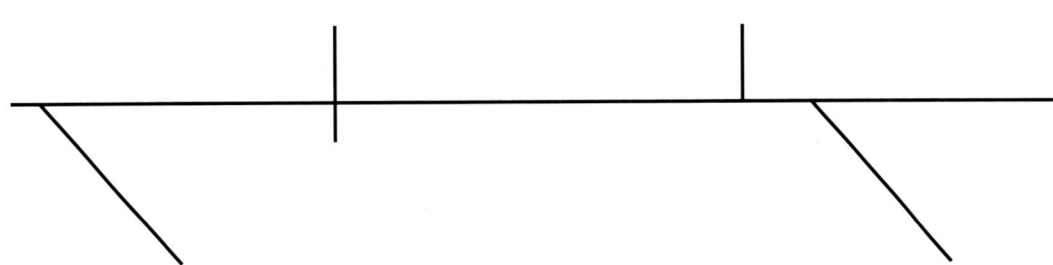

4. Horses eat oats.

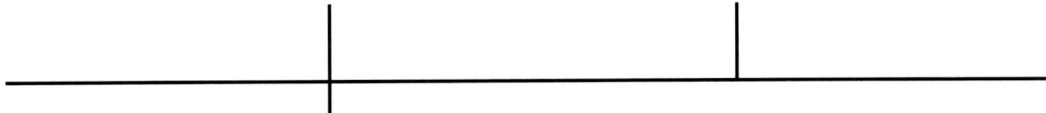

5. Valery made the bed.

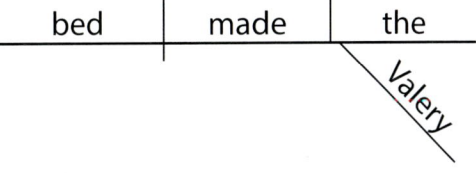

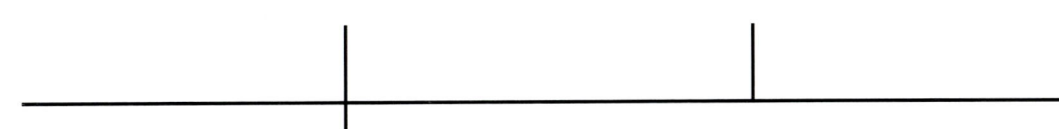

Direct Objects 13

DIAGRAMMING Level 1

ADJECTIVES

Adjectives are words that modify nouns. For example, we are not using just a workbook; we are using **this** (**limiting adjective**) workbook. As mentioned earlier, the articles the, a, and an, are also limiting adjectives. Additionally, it isn't just a wheelbarrow; it is **a** (**limiting adjective**) **red** (**descriptive adjective**) wheel barrow. Also, the man is not just a priest; he is **a** (**limiting adjective**) **Catholic** (**proper adjective**) priest. Finally, **possessive nouns** can also act as **adjective modifiers**. It is not just a tool; it is **Mike's** tool.

To diagram an **adjective**, place it on a slanted line underneath the noun that it modifies.

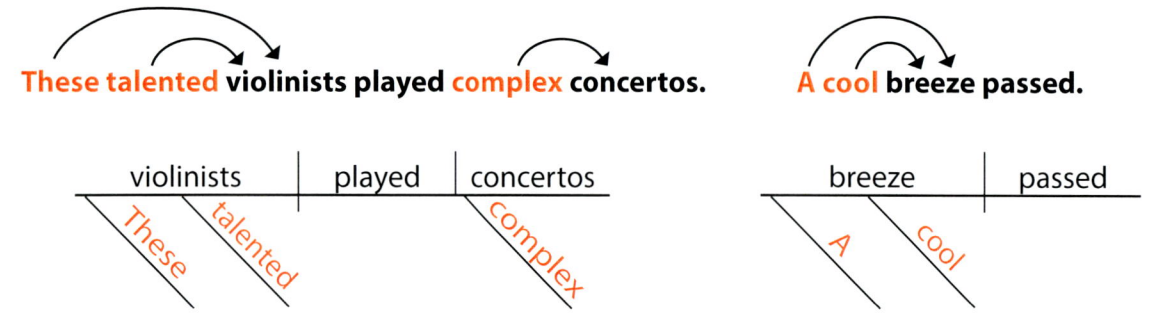

Exercise 1

In the following sentences, underline the adjectives once and circle the nouns they modify. Then diagram each sentence.

1. The large balloon floated.

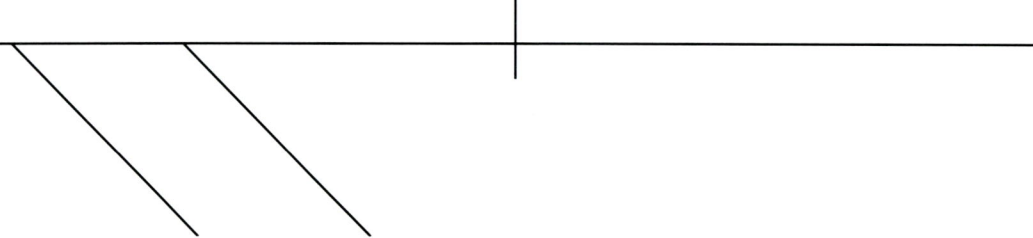

2. The French knight left the palace.

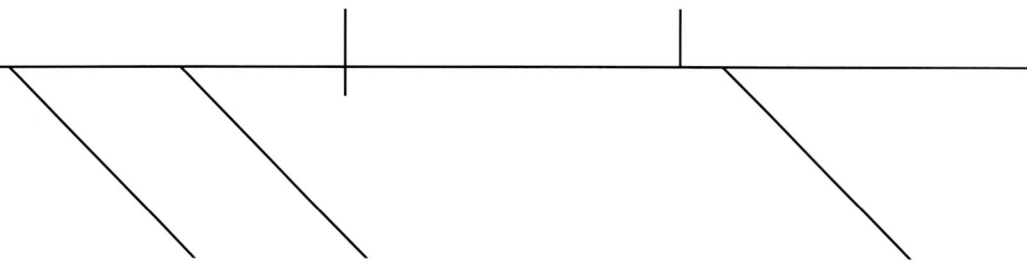

14 Adjectives

Name

DIAGRAMMING Level 1

3. That prized horse won the race.

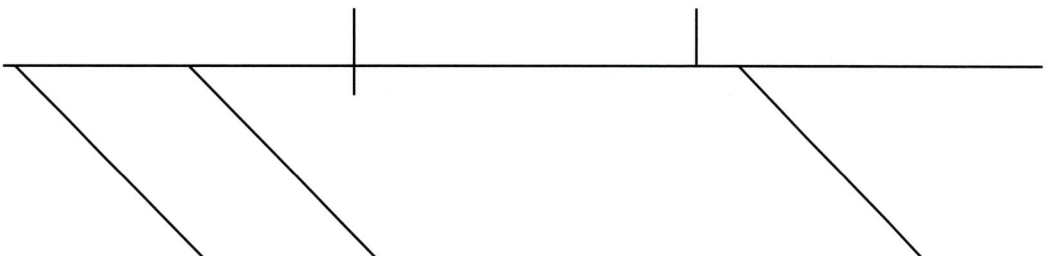

4. A beautiful flower bloomed.

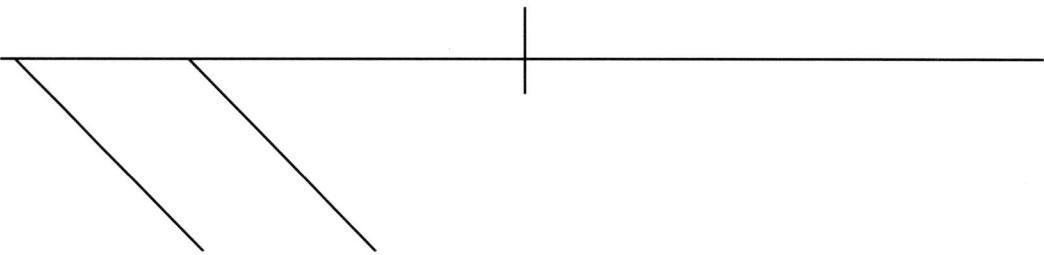

5. The successful doctor spoke.

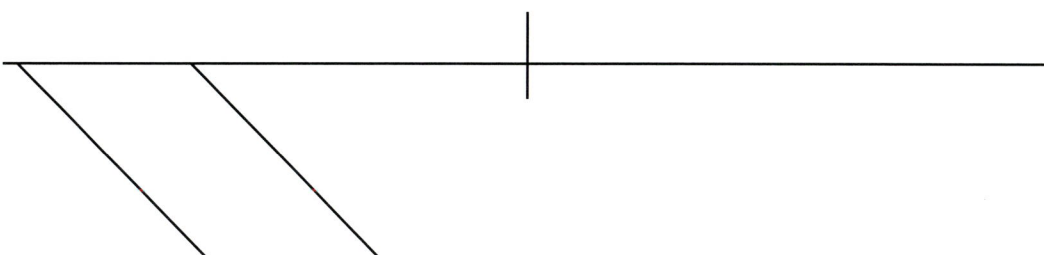

6. Tom's ship sailed the Atlantic coastline.

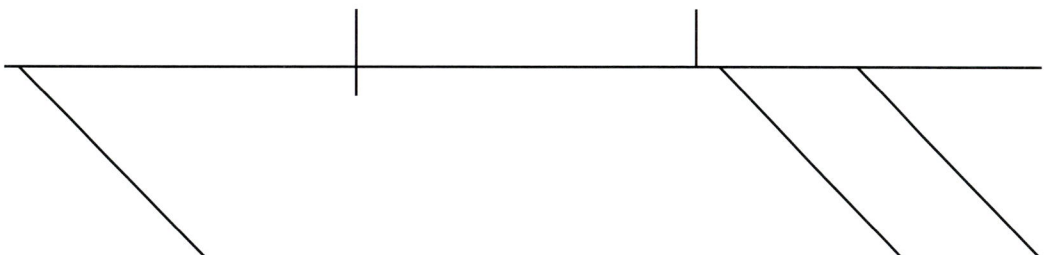

Adjectives 15

DIAGRAMMING Level 1

7. The expensive glove disappeared.

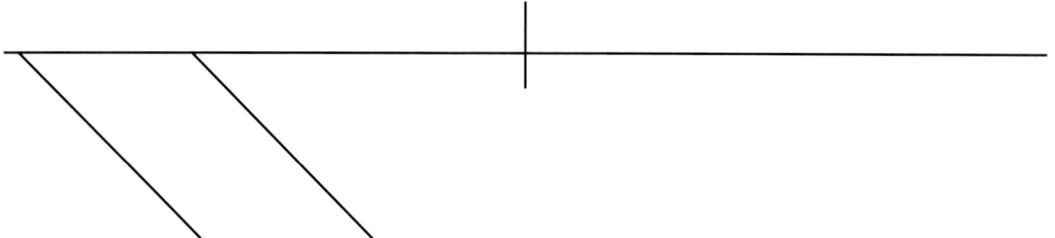

8. The kind uncle arrived.

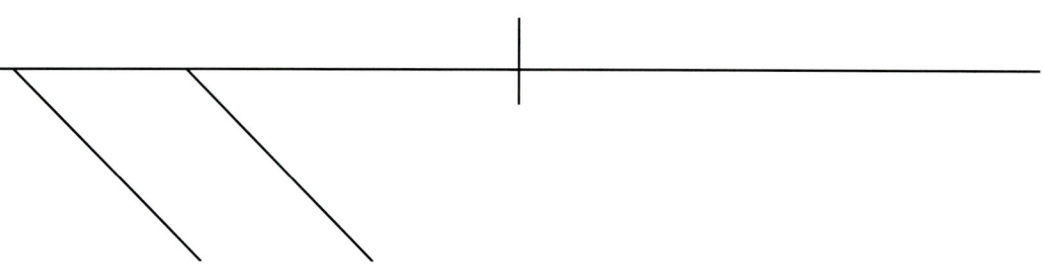

9. A lightning bolt split a tree.

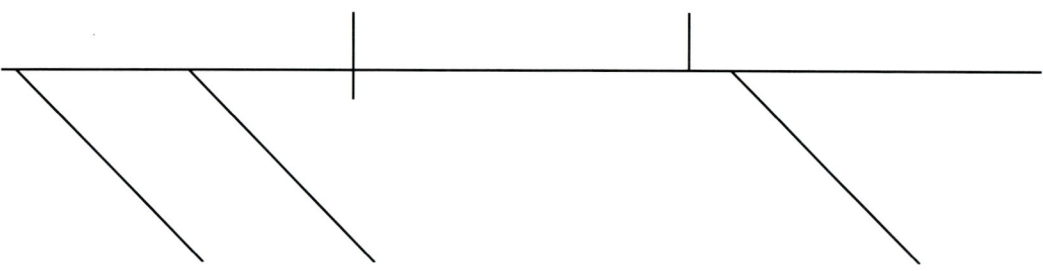

10. Angry politicians argue.

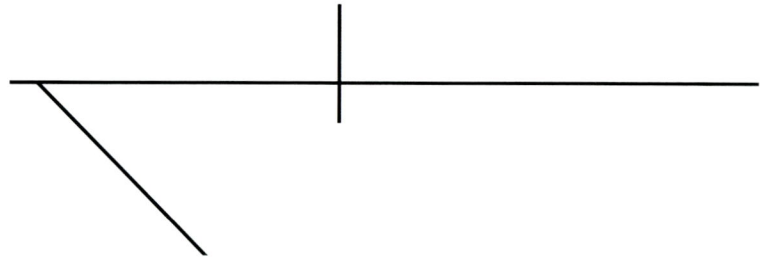

Name

DIAGRAMMING Level 1

Exercise 2

Create sentences with adjectives to fit these diagrams. Then write each one on the correct diagram.

1.

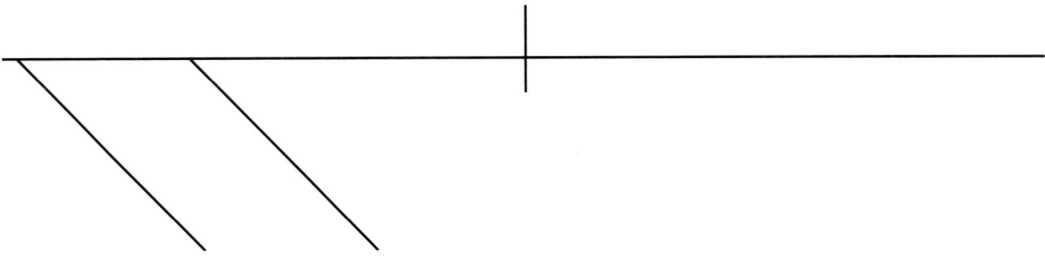

2.

3.

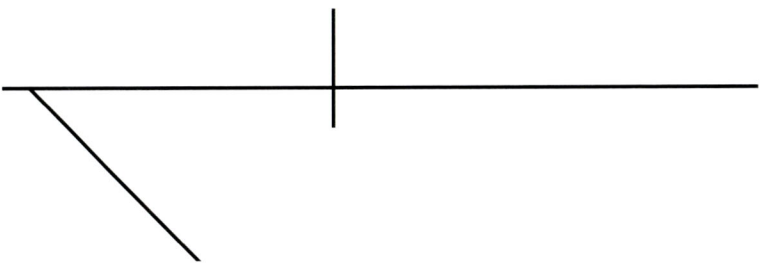

Adjectives 17

DIAGRAMMING Level 1

4.

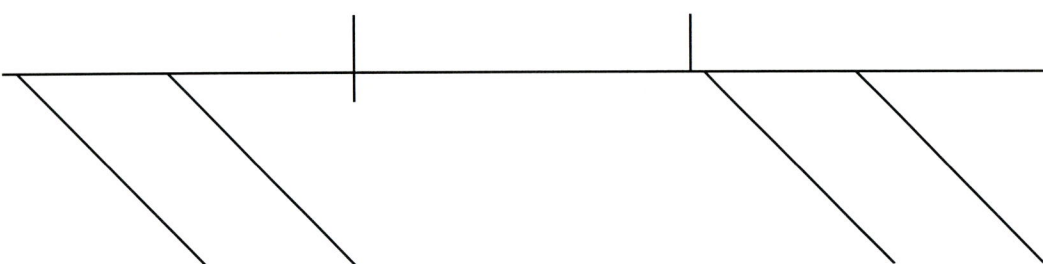

5.

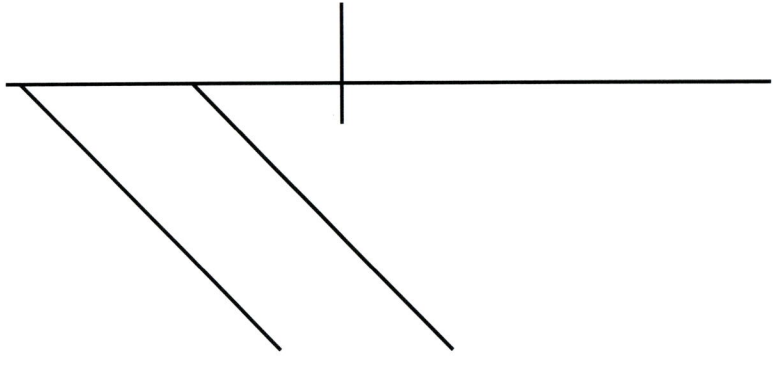

Exercise 3
Unscramble the groups of words to make complete sentences. Write the sentences on the blank lines. Then diagram them.

1. negotiated officer the police _____

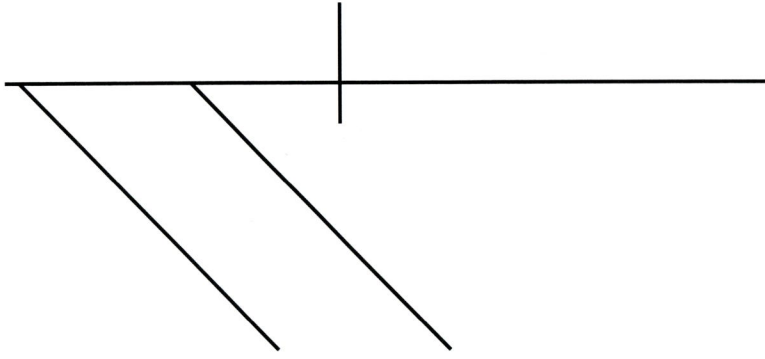

Name

DIAGRAMMING Level 1

2. skillful a performed monologue the actor

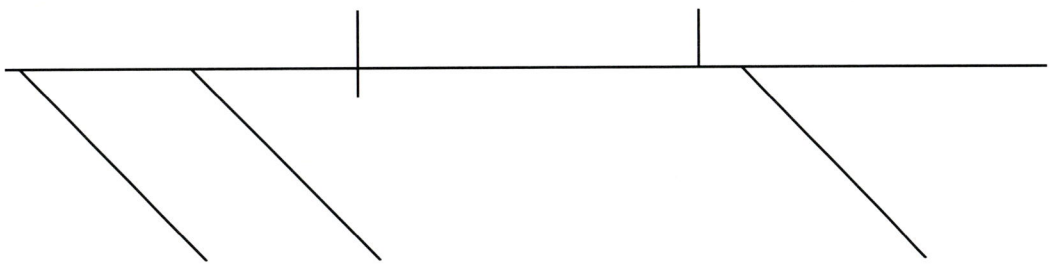

3. rumbled red the truck

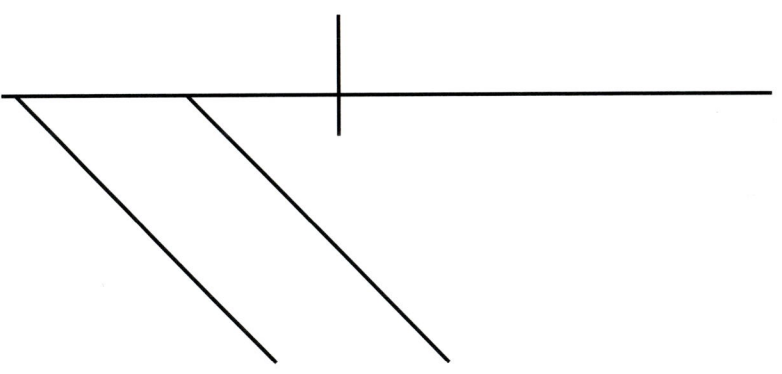

4. sick the Jesus healed man

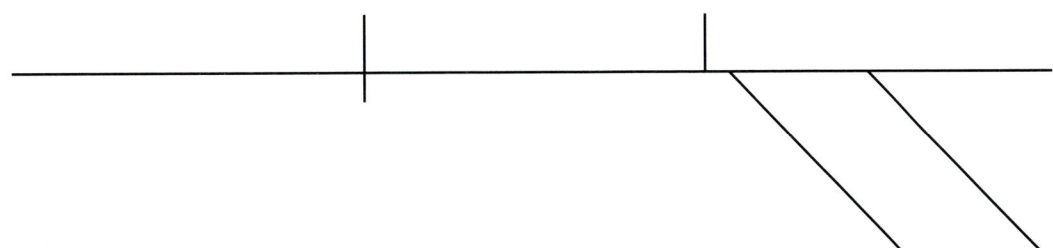

DIAGRAMMING Level 1

5. matches the continued tennis _____

Exercise 4

Find the mistakes in the following diagrams. Then, diagram the sentences correctly on the given, blank diagrams. Note: you may need to fix the blank diagram by drawing a new line(s).

1. **Miriam's basket fell.**

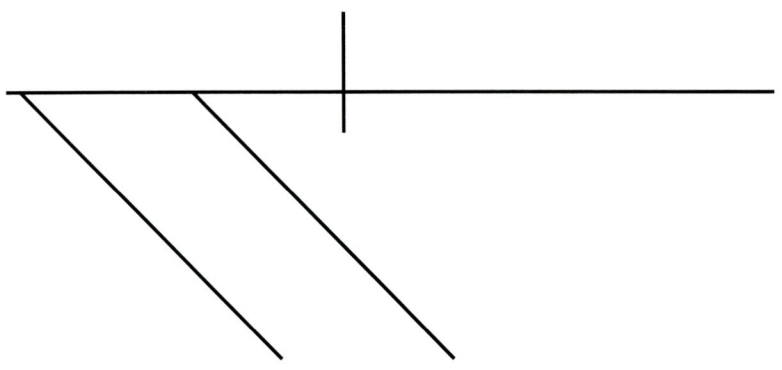

2. **A race car drifted.**

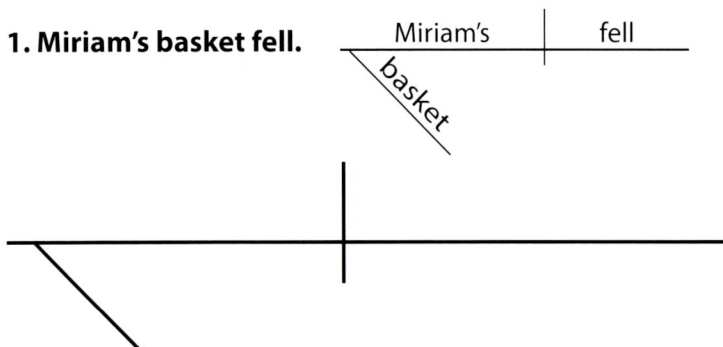

Name

3. The tired children did the chores.

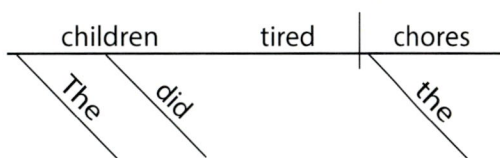
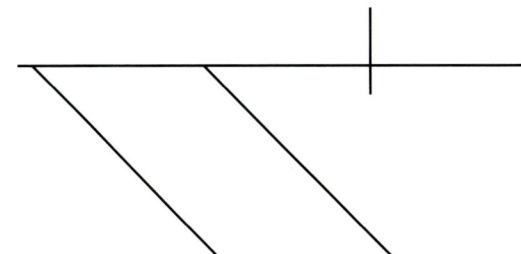

4. A barn owl hooted.

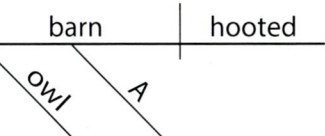

5. The Siamese cat swatted the shiny mirror.

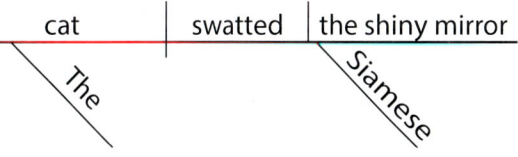

DIAGRAMMING Level 1

SUBJECTIVE COMPLEMENTS

A noun or pronoun that follows a linking verb and is the same person, place, or thing as the **subject** is a **subjective complement**. An **adjective** can also be a **subjective complement** because it can describe the **subject**. Examples of **linking verbs** are *am*, *is*, *are*, *was*, *were*, *be*, and *been*.

Diagram a **subjective complement** by placing it on the same line as the **subject** and **predicate**. Separate the **predicate** from the **subjective complement** by drawing a line that slants back toward the **subject** it describes.

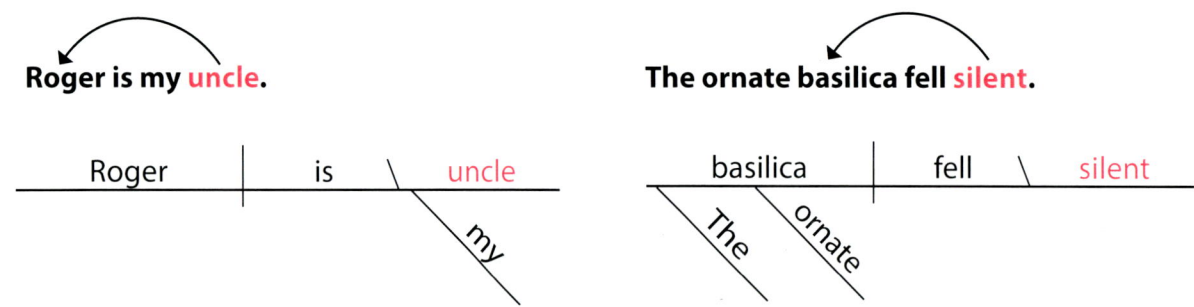

Exercise 1

In the following sentences, underline the subjective complements once and circle the nouns they complement. Then diagram each sentence.

1. Mary is a skilled doctor.

2. This English class is amazing.

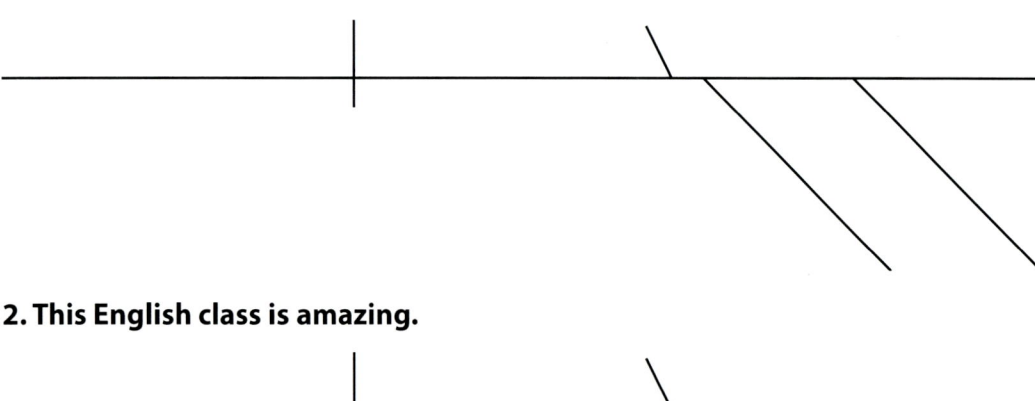

22 Subjective Complements

Name

DIAGRAMMING Level 1

3. He became a saint.

4. Sean was the class president.

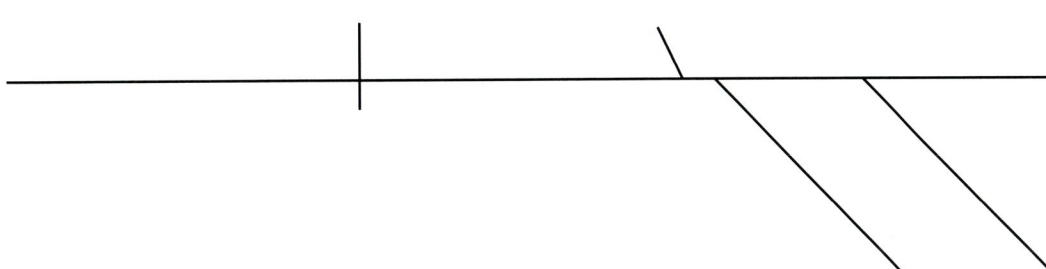

5. We grew sleepy.

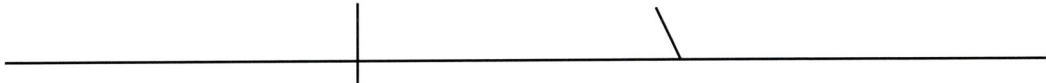

6. The dog was a puppy.

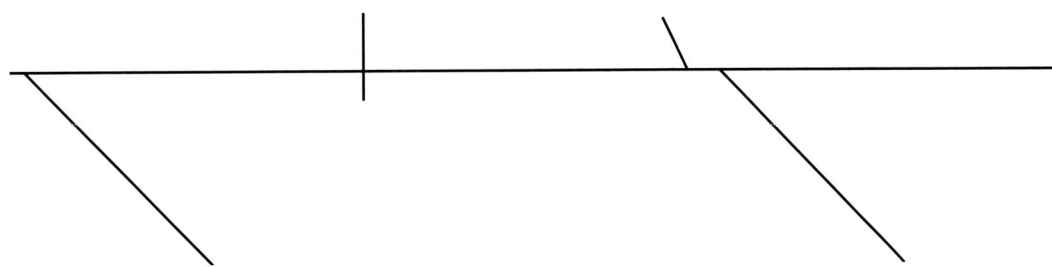

Subjective Complements 23

DIAGRAMMING Level 1

7. The beach is crowded.

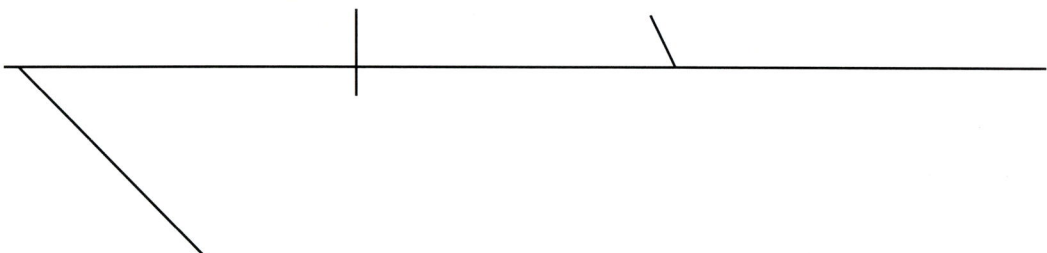

8. It is she.

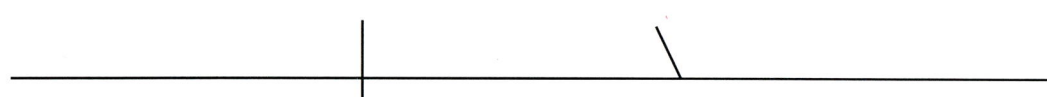

9. I am the captain.

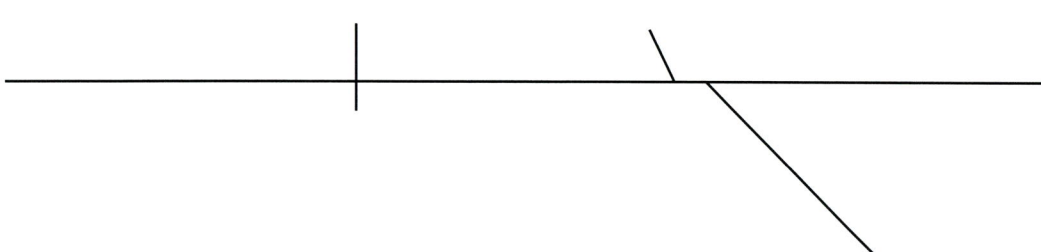

10. That woman is Jean's mom.

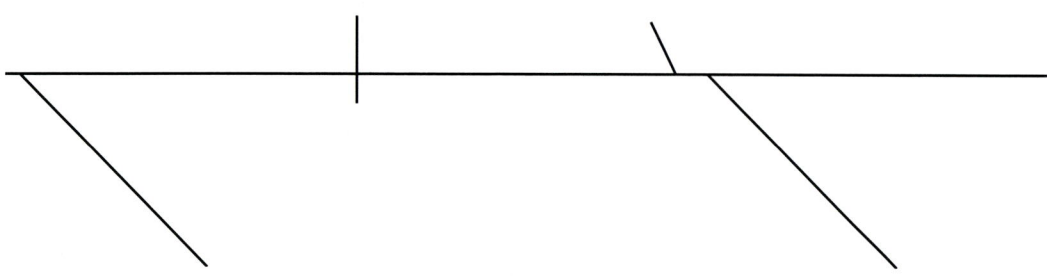

DIAGRAMMING Level 1

Name

Exercise 2

Create sentences with a subjective complement to fit these diagrams. Then write each one on the correct diagram.

1.

2.

3.

DIAGRAMMING Level 1

4.

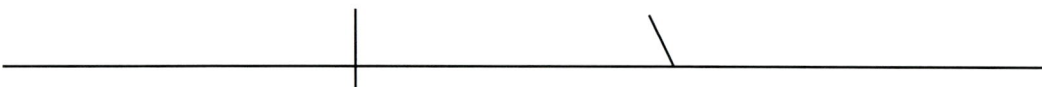

5.

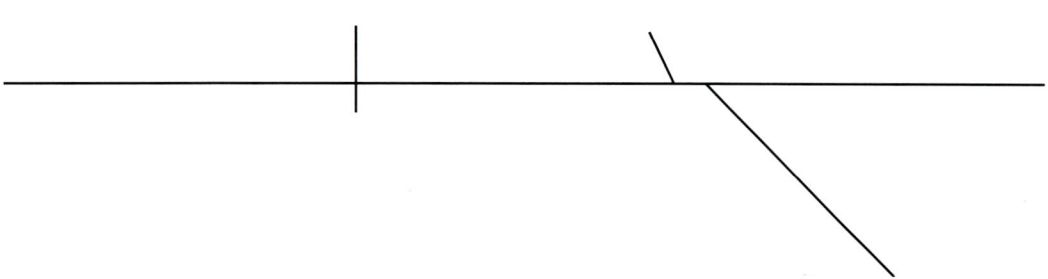

Exercise 3

Unscramble the groups of words to make complete sentences. Write the sentences on the blank lines. Then diagram them.

1. a Nathan student is college _____

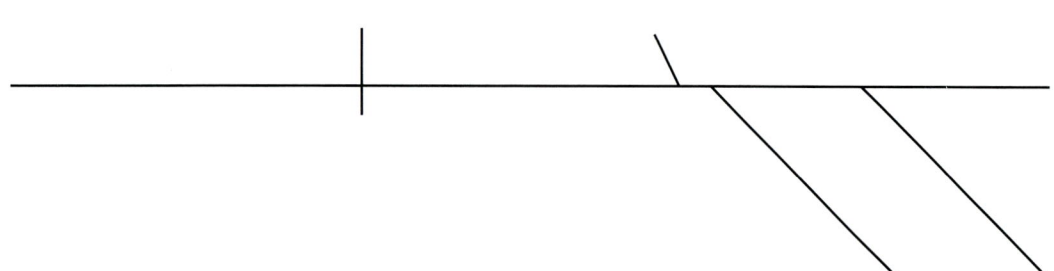

DIAGRAMMING Level 1

Name

2. expensive classical are instruments

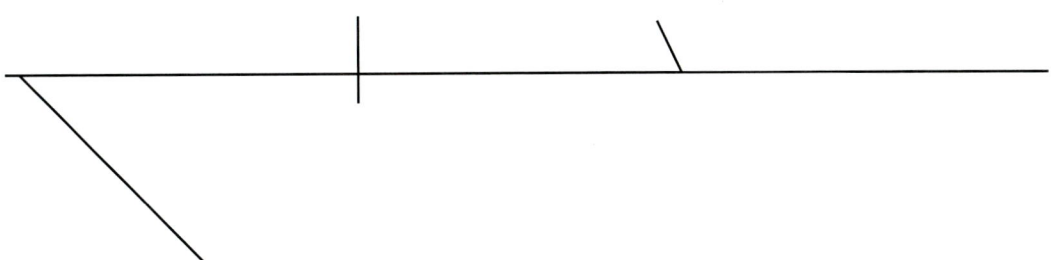

3. English St. George was

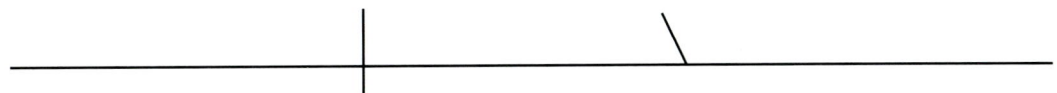

4. entertaining a good is movie

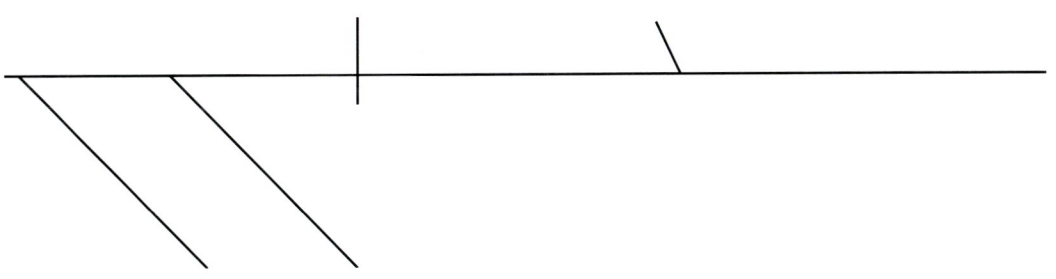

5. man lawyer was a this

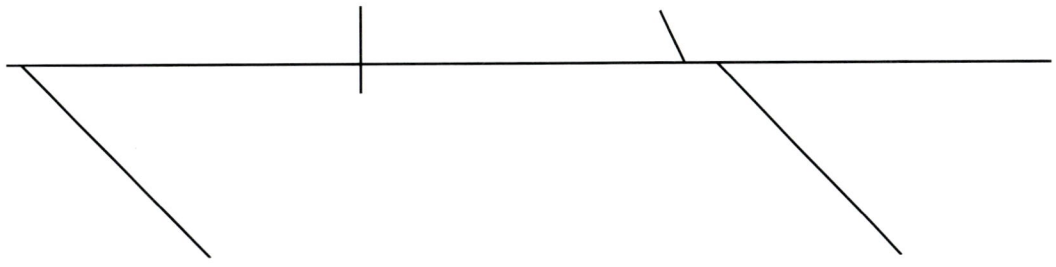

Subjective Complements

DIAGRAMMING Level 1

Exercise 4

Find the mistakes in the following diagrams. Then, diagram the sentences correctly on the given, blank diagrams. Note: you may need to fix the blank diagram by drawing a new line(s).

1. Veronica is the best dancer.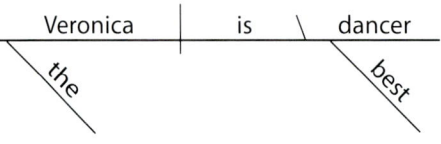

2. The forest trail was beautiful.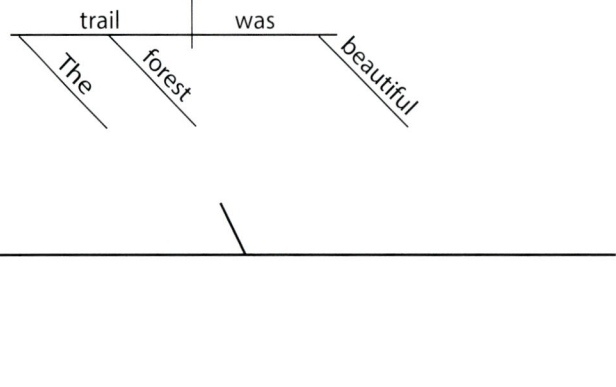

3. The swans were old.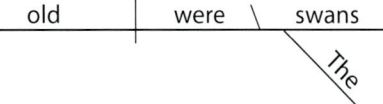

28 Subjective Complements

Name

4. Gene is a poet.

5. Pope St. John Paul II was a holy man.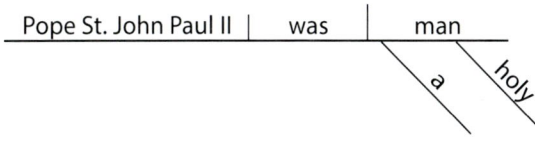

DIAGRAMMING Level 1

VERB PHRASES

Sometimes the predicate is a **verb phrase**. A *verb phrase* does the *work of a single verb* and is made of two parts: one or more **helping verbs** and a **main verb**.

1.) **Helping verbs** include *can, will, were, have, did, would* or *should*. (For a more extensive list of helping verbs, refer to an English grammar book.)

2.) The **main verb** is the last verb in the **verb phrase**. **Main verbs** can be either **being verbs** or **action verbs**.

2a.) Examples of a **verb phrase** with a **helping verb** and **being verb** are *will be, can be, have been,* or *would be*.

2b.) **Action verbs** are any verbs that express action such as, *sings, jumps, throws, thinks,* or *sleeps*. Examples of a **verb phrase** with a **helping verb** and an **action verb** are *can pray, will build,* and *did know*.

It is important to note that **linking verbs** have **subjective complements** and **action verbs** have **direct objects**. See the examples below.

Jesse will be an electrician.   **The farm could grow corn.**

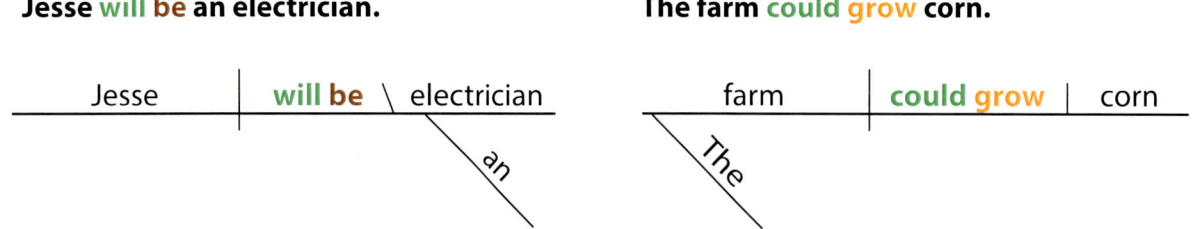

Exercise 1

In the following sentences, underline the helping verbs once and circle the being or action verbs in the following verb phrases. Then diagram each sentence.

1. The church could be a cathedral.

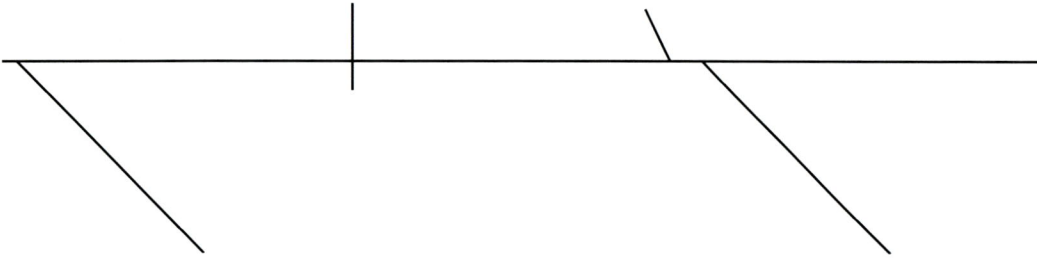

30   Verb Phrases

Name

DIAGRAMMING Level 1

2. James has given money.

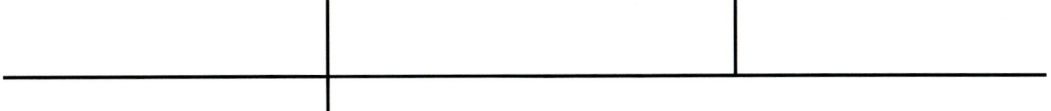

3. The camp must be fun

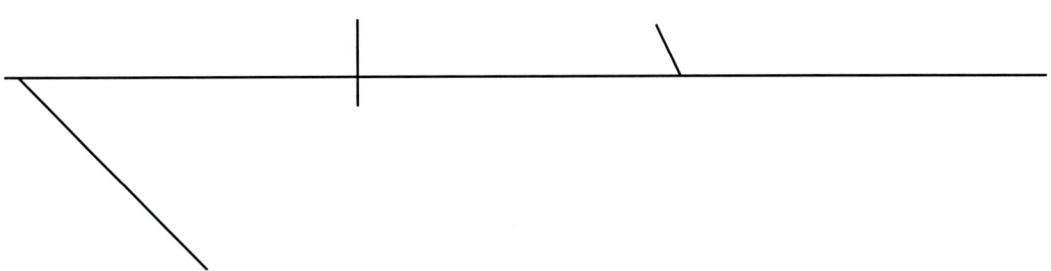

4. The surf board will be white.

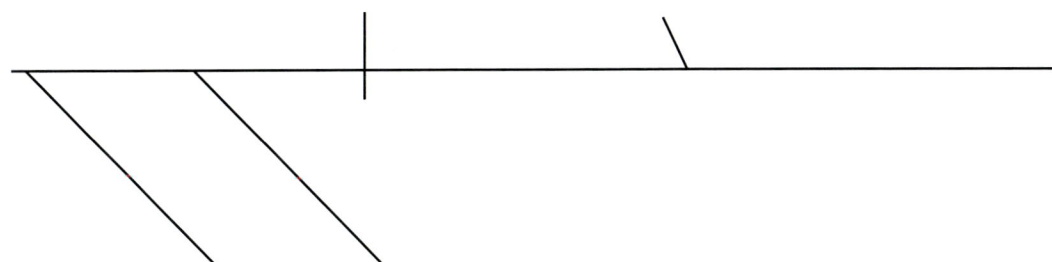

5. The painter might donate a painting.

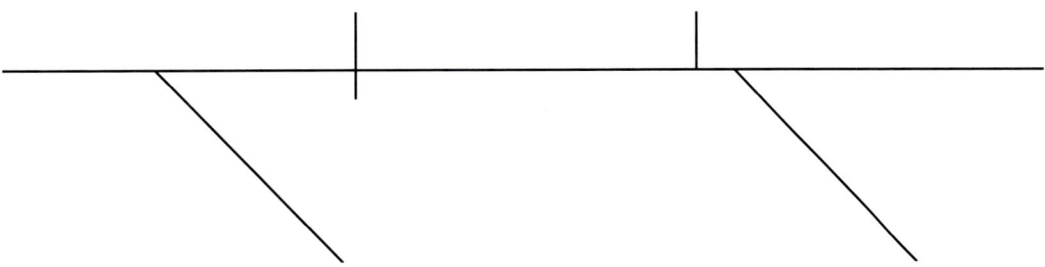

Verb Phrases 31

DIAGRAMMING Level 1

Exercise 2

Create one sentence with a helping verb, being verb, and subjective complement. Create another sentence with a helping verb, action verb, and direct object.

1.

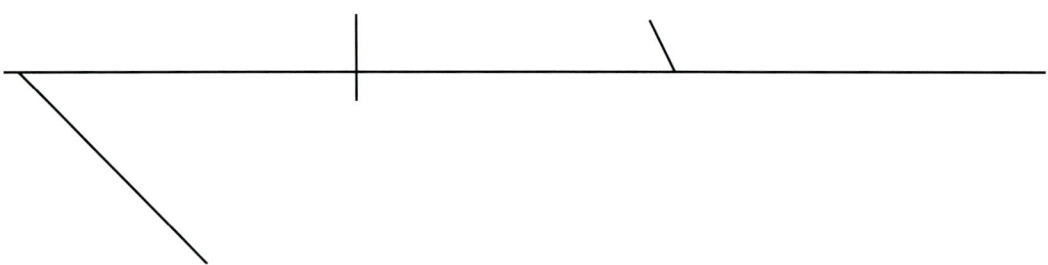

2.

Name _____

DIAGRAMMING Level 1

ADVERBS (TIME, PLACE, AND MANNER)

An **adverb** is a word that modifies a **verb, adjective,** or another **adverb**. In this workbook, we will only look at how **adverbs** modify **verbs** in sentences.

For example: It will not only snow; it will snow **soon** (**adverb of time**). He doesn't only run; he runs **outside** (**adverb of place**). You do not simply ride your bike; you **quickly** (**adverb of manner**) ride your bike.

To diagram an **adverb**, draw a slanted line underneath the verb it modifies. Notice the similarity between diagramming **adverbs** and the earlier section on **adjectives**.

Note: *Sometimes adverbs are not found right after the verb. To determine if a word is an adverb, ask yourself, "Is this word describing when, where, how often, or in what manner the predicate/verb is being done?"*

John left first.

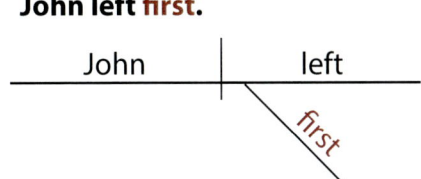

The angry bobcat lunged forward.

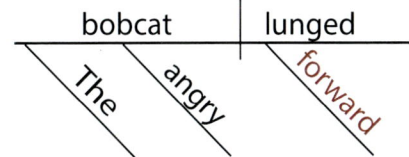

Exercise 1

In the following sentences, underline the adverbs once and circle the predicates they modify. Then diagram each sentence.

1. Father Simon will celebrate Mass tomorrow.

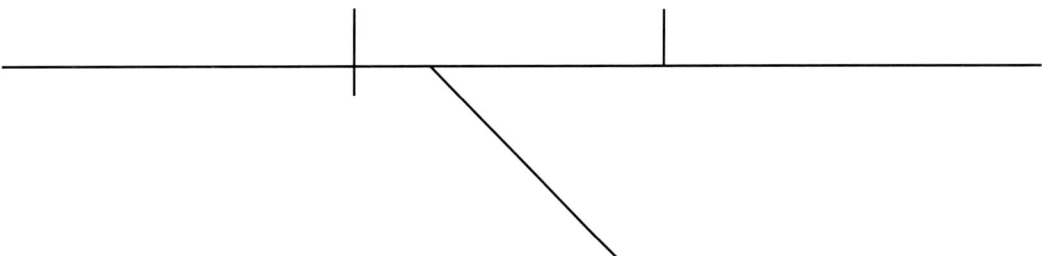

2. Modern toasters provide heat rapidly.

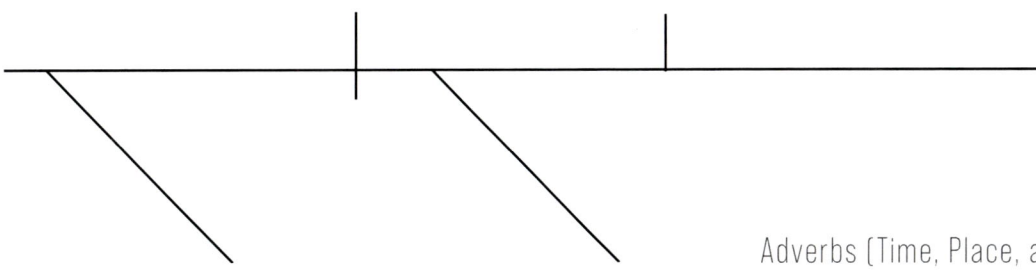

Adverbs (Time, Place, and Manner) 33

DIAGRAMMING Level 1

3. Harry stumbled ahead.

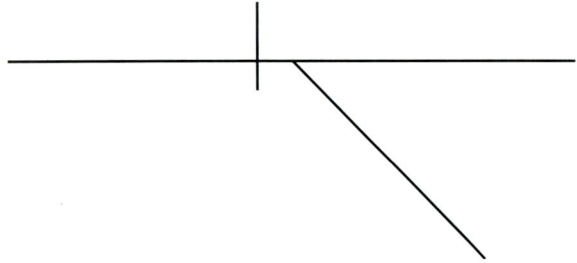

4. Virginia's weather can change suddenly.

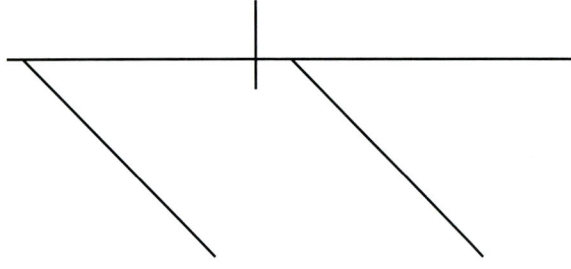

5. We will watch today.

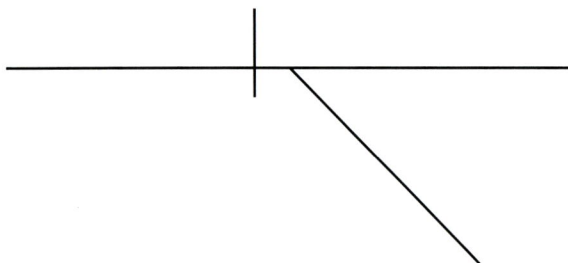

6. The sun shone brightly.

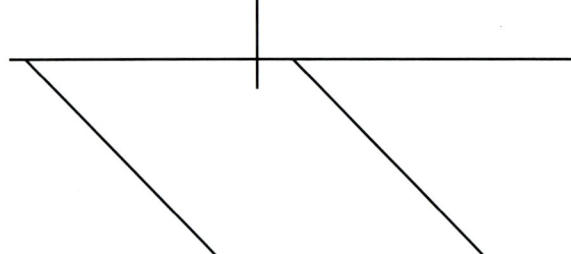

Name

DIAGRAMMING Level 1

7. The incense floated upward.

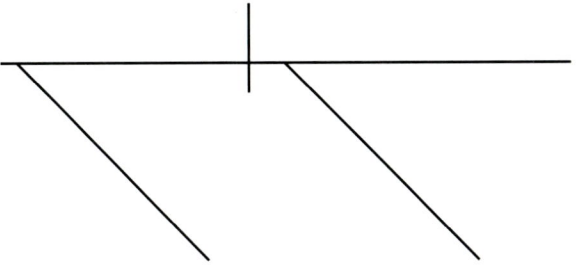

8. Jesus knew the man well.

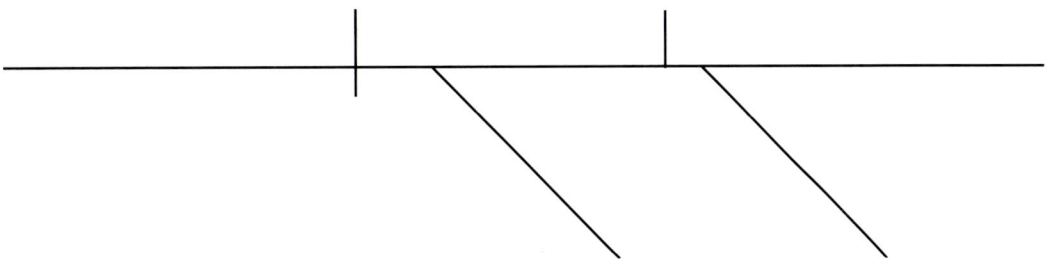

9. Jason reads frequently.

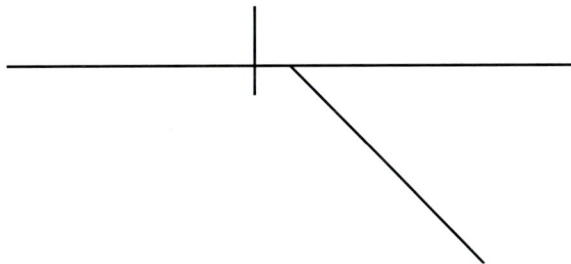

10. The dangerous blizzard blew snow everywhere.

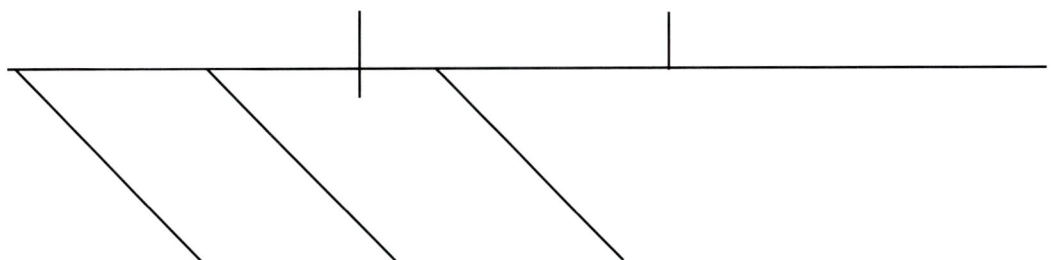

Adverbs (Time, Place, and Manner) 35

DIAGRAMMING Level 1

Exercise 2

Create sentences with adverbs to fit these diagrams. Then write each one on the correct diagram.

1.

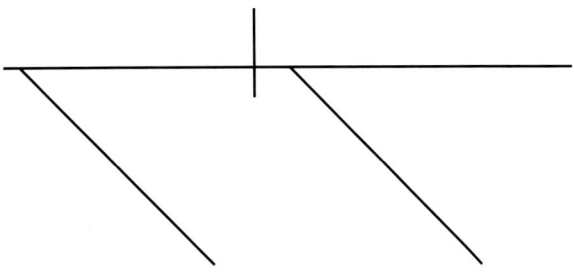

2.

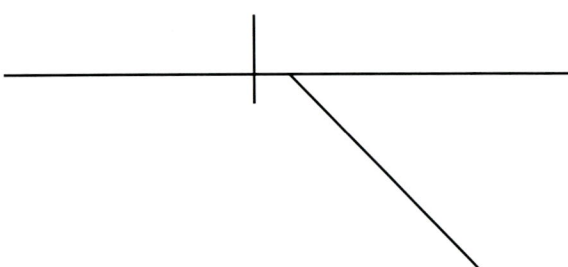

3.

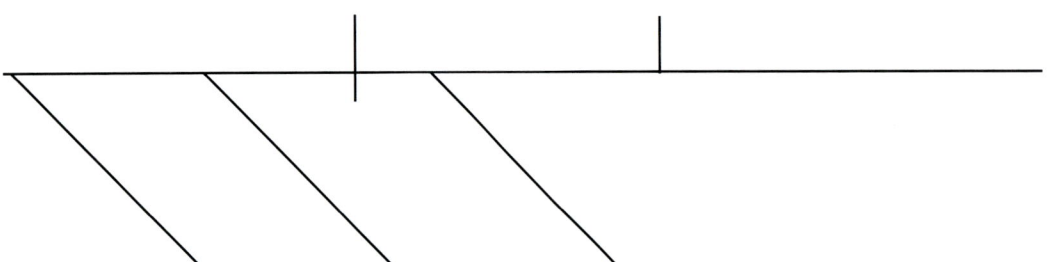

Name

DIAGRAMMING Level 1

4.

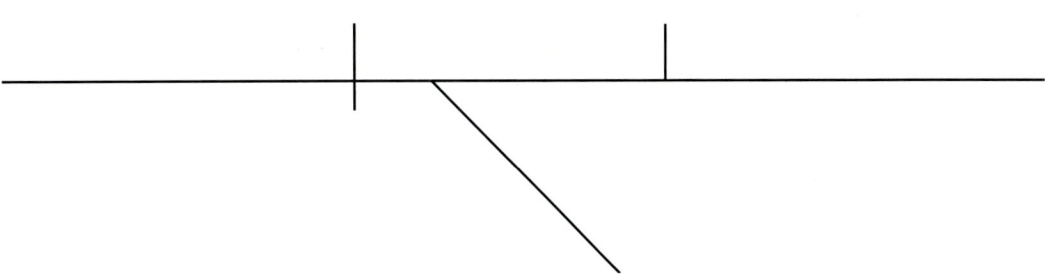

5.

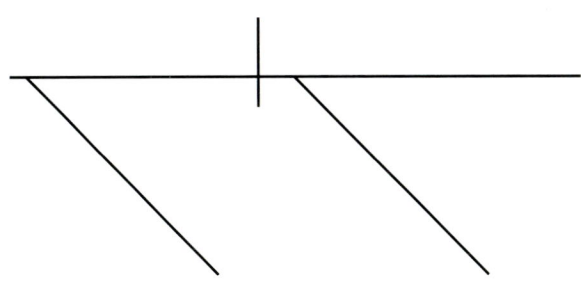

Exercise 3

Unscramble the groups of words to make complete sentences. Write the sentences on the blank lines. Then diagram them.

1. horse eagerly Victoria bridled her _____

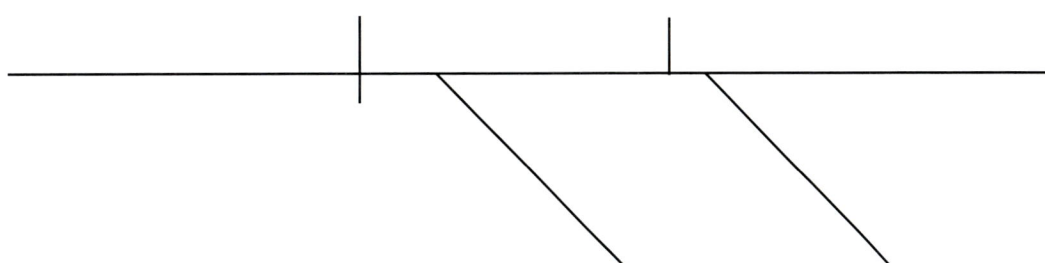

Adverbs (Time, Place, and Manner)

DIAGRAMMING Level 1

2. the below flew falcon

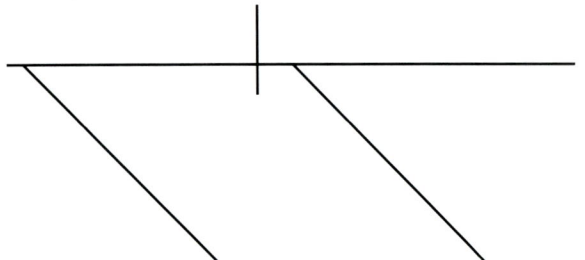

3. rudely man the shouted

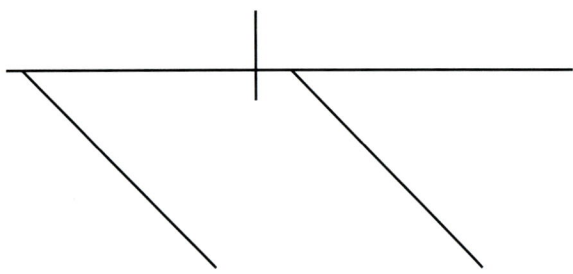

4. usually the prays Samuel Rosary

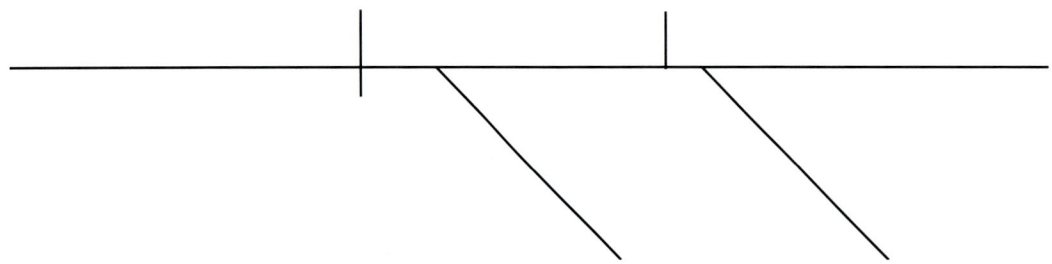

Adverbs (Time, Place, and Manner)

Name _____

DIAGRAMMING Level 1

5. clouds the approached dark quickly _____

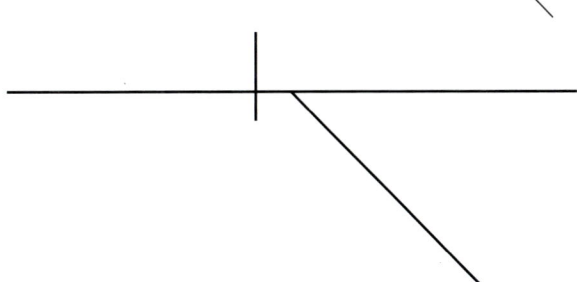

Exercise 4

Find the mistakes in the following diagrams. Then, diagram the sentences correctly on the given, blank diagrams. Note: you may need to fix the blank diagram by drawing a new line(s).

1. She called within.

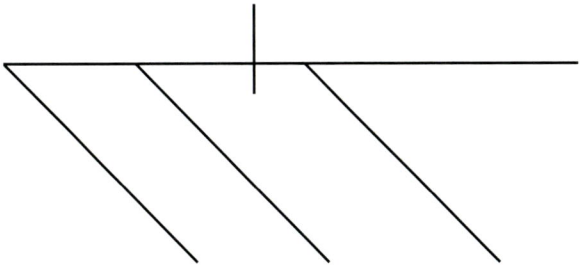

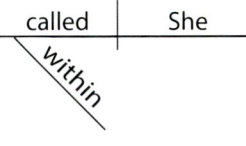

2. The butler often writes notes.

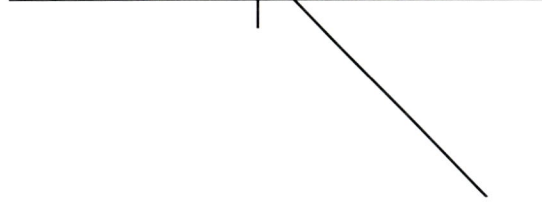

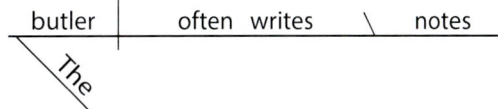

Adverbs (Time, Place, and Manner) **39**

DIAGRAMMING Level 1

3. Sam dropped the weights roughly.

4. Soon, I will have a good grade.

5. The saints lived bravely.

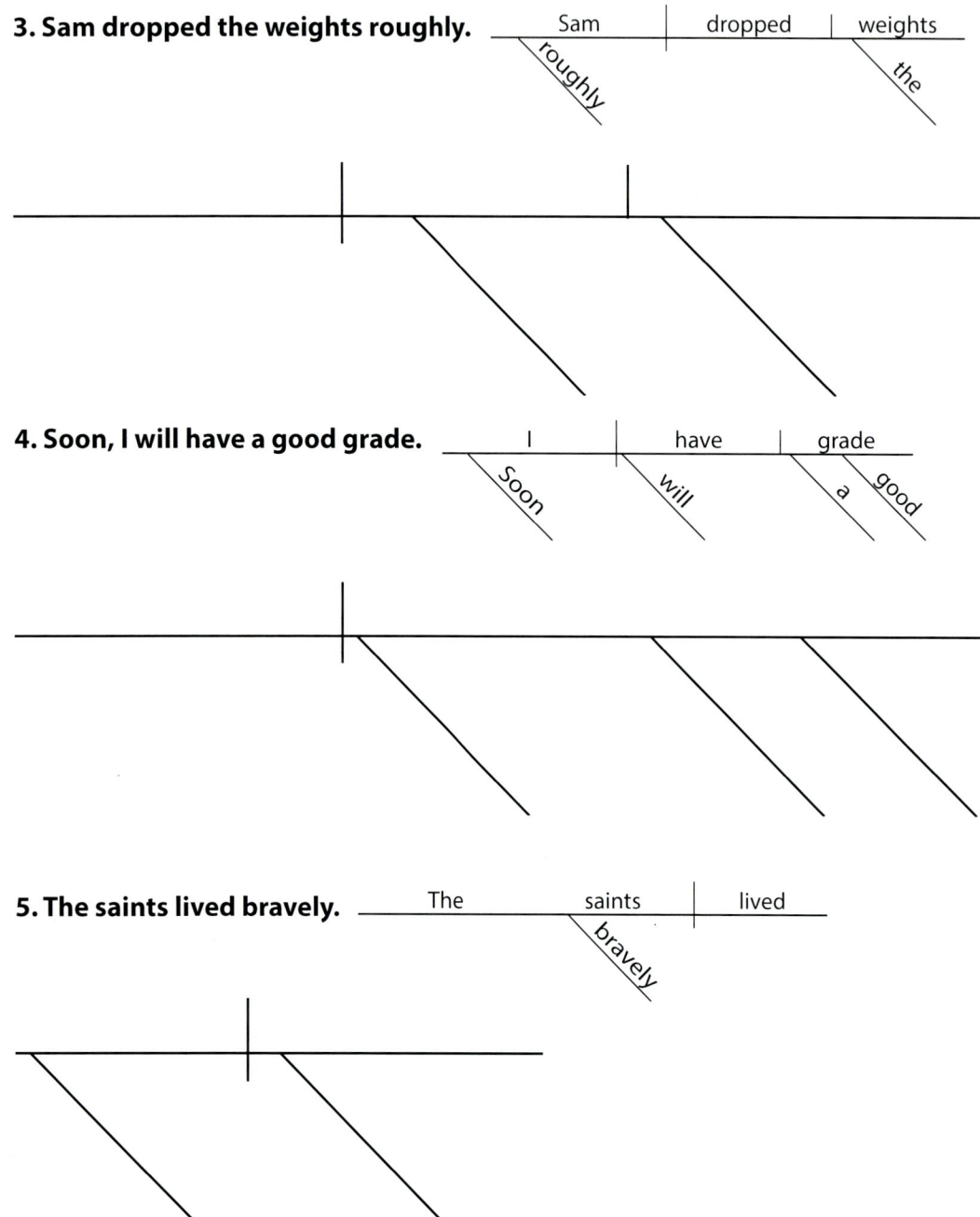

Adverbs (Time, Place, and Manner)

Name

DIAGRAMMING Level 1

COMPOUND PREDICATES

In the first section, you learned how the verb expresses action or being and that the verb functions as the **predicate** of the sentence. Some predicates of the sentence have more than one verb or verb phrase; this is called a **compound predicate**. A compound predicate allows the **subject** to perform two actions. In order to connect the two verbs, sentences use the **conjunctions** *and*, *or*, and sometimes *but*.

To diagram a **compound predicate**, draw two parallel lines joined by diagonal lines to the horizontal line containing the **subject**. Write the **conjunction** on the dotted line between two verbs.

Forest fires burn and destroy homes.   Chelsea scuttled and scurried.

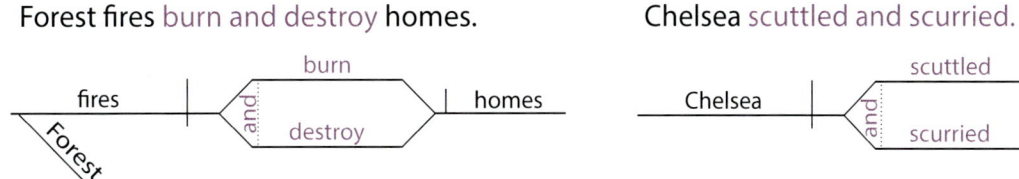

Exercise 1

In the following sentences, circle the verbs and conjunctions that make up the compound predicate. Then diagram each sentence.

1. Bob knows and loves God.

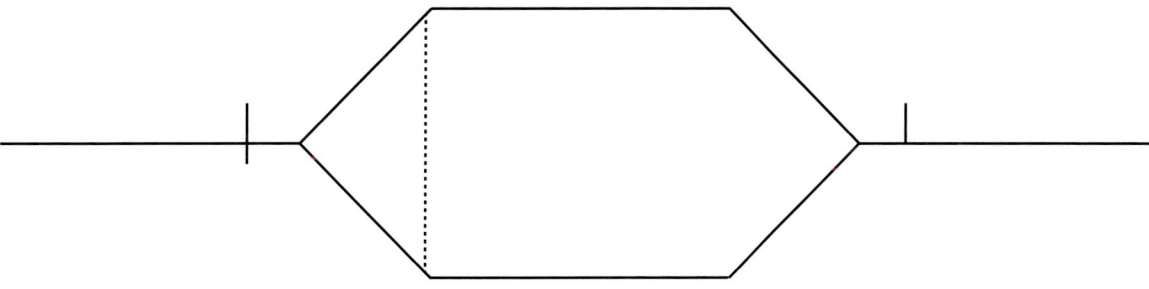

2. Math challenges and improves the mind.

Compound Predicates 41

DIAGRAMMING Level 1

3. Isabelle cooked and baked.

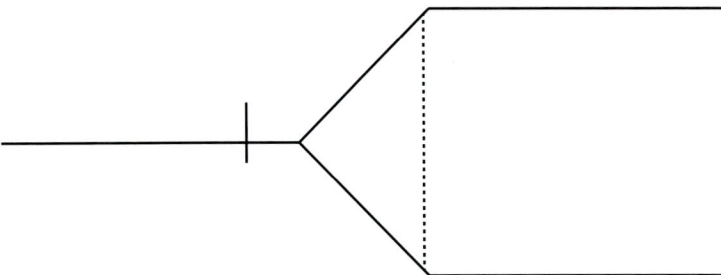

4. I win or lose.

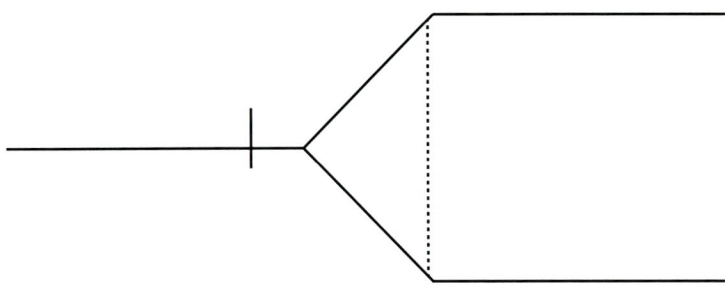

5. St. Thérèse lived and preached a simple life.

6. The red bowl fell and smashed.

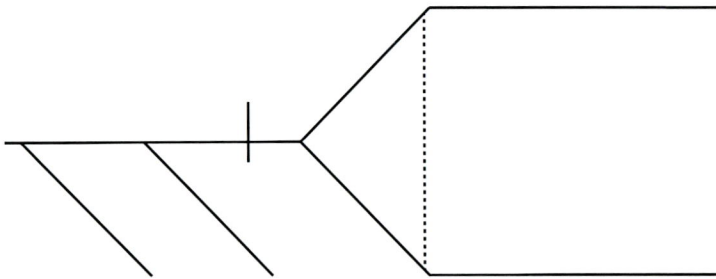

Name

7. Water hydrates and cools.

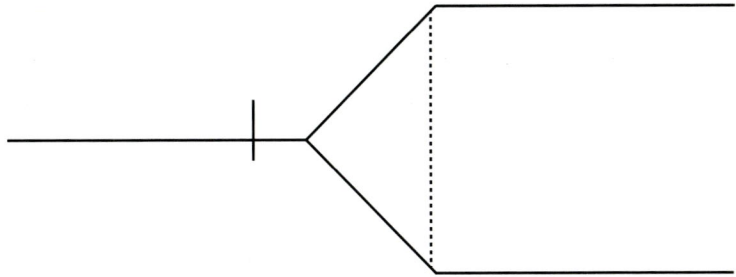

8. Chris lifted and shoved the box.

9. Tamara learns and remembers people's names.

10. A computer hummed and flickered.

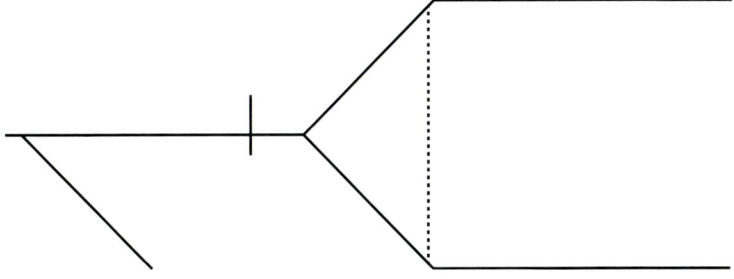

DIAGRAMMING Level 1

Exercise 2
Create sentences with a compound predicate to fit these diagrams. Then write each one on the correct diagram.

1.

2.
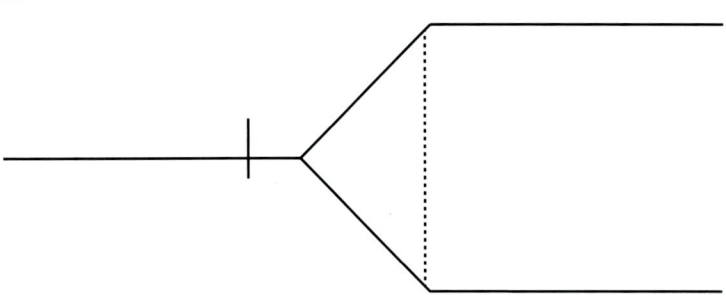

3.
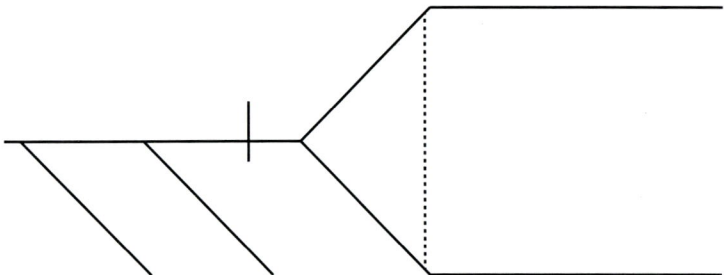

4.

44 Compound Predicates

Name _____

DIAGRAMMING Level 1

5.

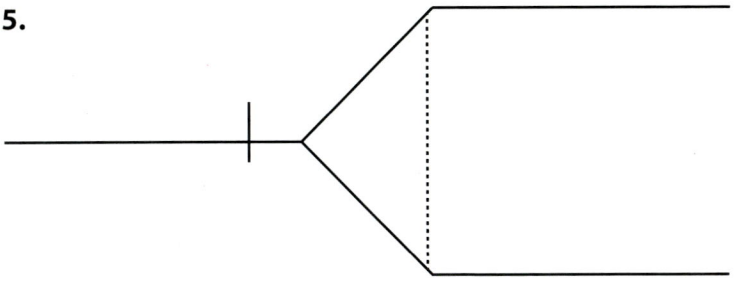

Exercise 3

Unscramble the groups of words to make a complete sentence. Write the sentences on the blank lines. Then diagram them.

1. caught Bernadette and threw the ball _____

2. excited and the sprinted athlete shouted _____

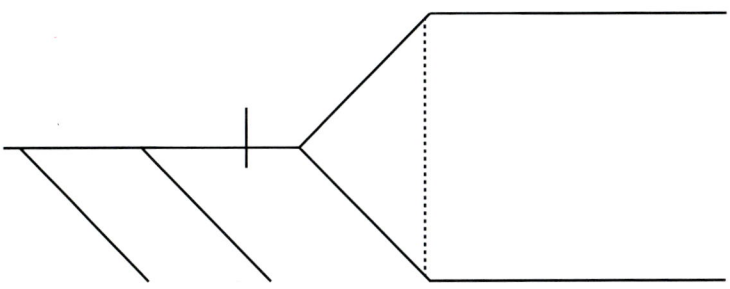

Compound Predicates **45**

DIAGRAMMING Level 1

3. firemen saved residents and the rescued the_____

4. jumped and the danced girls _____

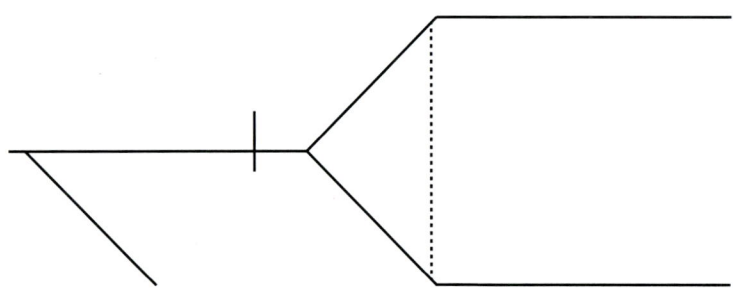

5. news Michael the and read absorbed_____

46 Compound Predicates

DIAGRAMMING Level 1

Name

Exercise 4

Find the mistakes in the following diagrams. Then, diagram the sentences correctly on the given, blank diagrams. Note: you may need to fix the blank diagram by drawing a new line(s).

1. The angry mob yelled and shouted.

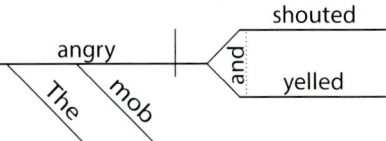

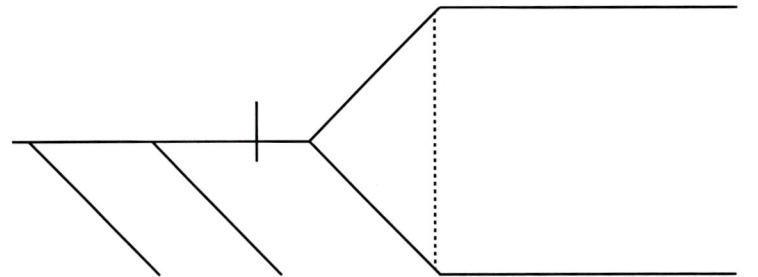

2. An altar boy lit and swung the censer.

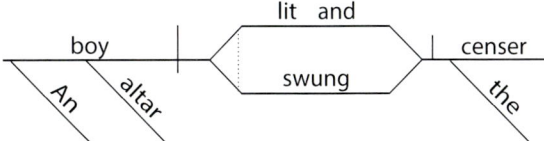

3. Luke entered and pointed.

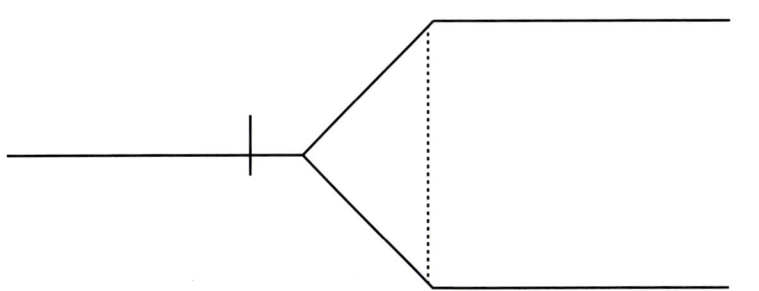

Compound Predicates 47

DIAGRAMMING Level 1

4. We dusted and organized our garage.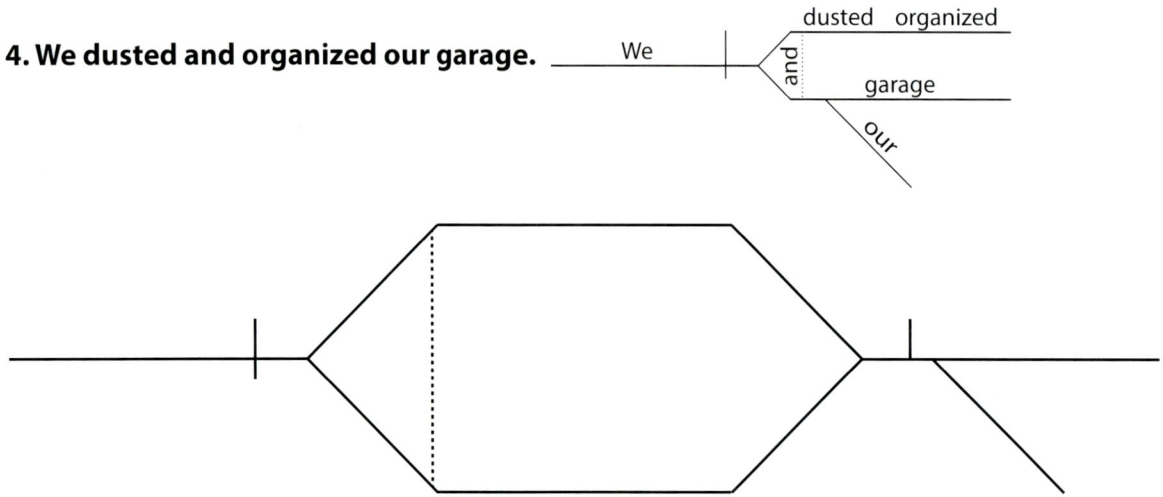

5. The large walrus slipped and splashed.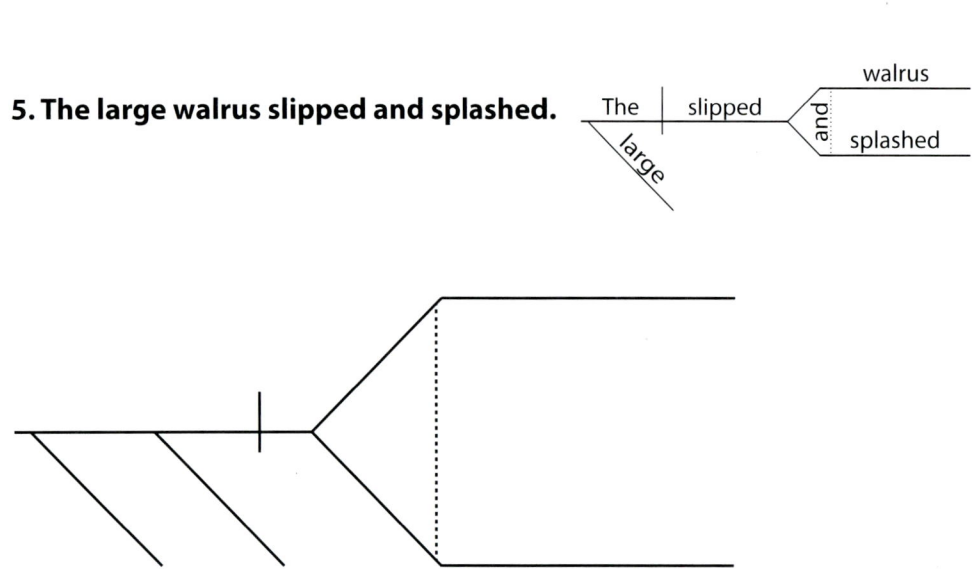

Compound Predicates

Name

DIAGRAMMING Level 1

COMPOUND SUBJECTS

In the first section of this book, you learned to find the **subject** by asking *who/what* is doing the action or being. A compound subject is composed of two or more subjects. In other words, two persons or things are doing the action or being.

To diagram a **compound subject**, draw a structure almost identical to a **compound predicate**: two parallel lines connected to a horizontal line containing the **predicate**. Remember to write the **conjunction** on a dotted line connecting the **subjects**.

Sam and Angela helped.

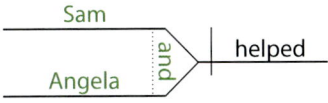

Heaven and hell are real.

Exercise 1

In the following sentences, circle the nouns, pronouns, adjectives, and conjunctions in the compound subject. Then diagram each sentence.

1. The turtles and fish swam away.

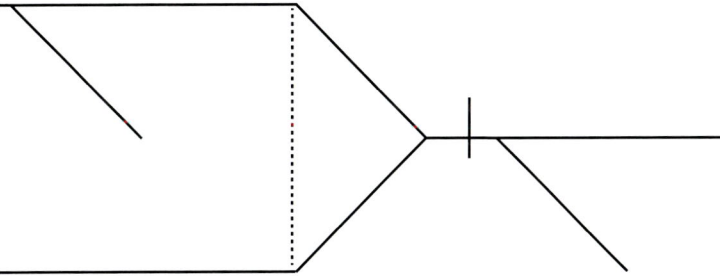

2. Mom and I prepared and baked two cakes.

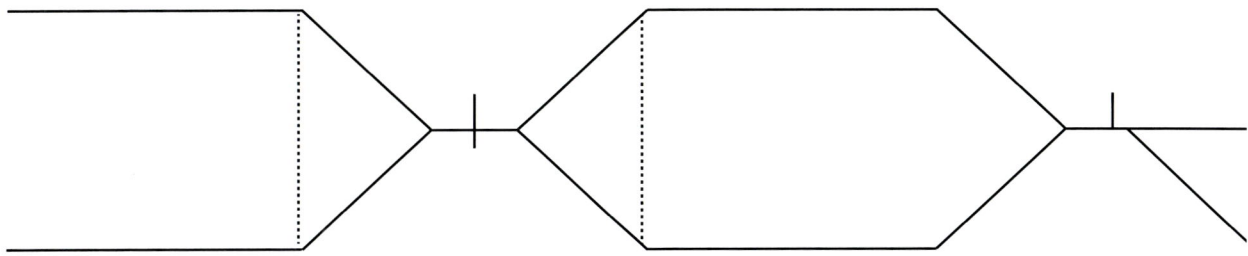

Compound Subjects 49

DIAGRAMMING Level 1

3. The plants and the fields are beautiful.

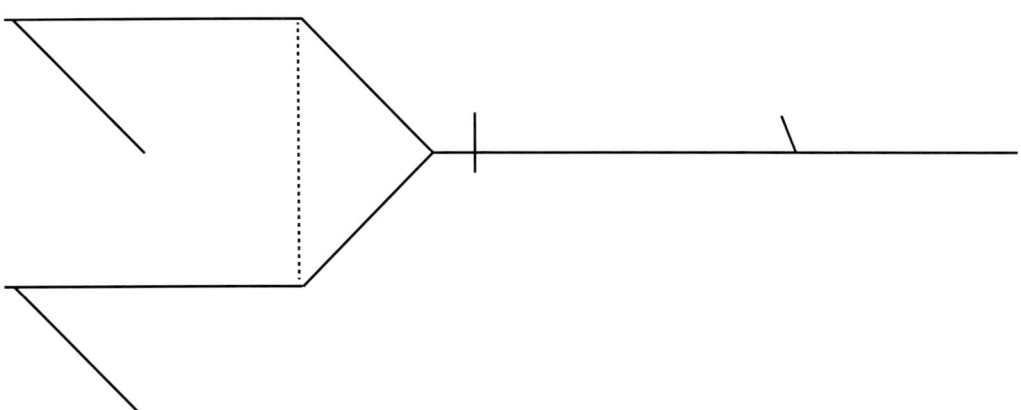

4. Harriet and Thomas slowly walked.

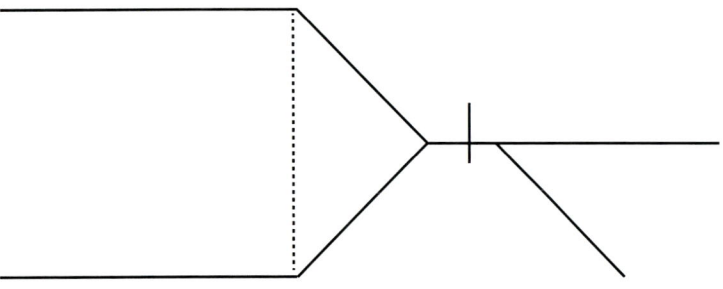

5. A hickory branch and an oak tree fell suddenly.

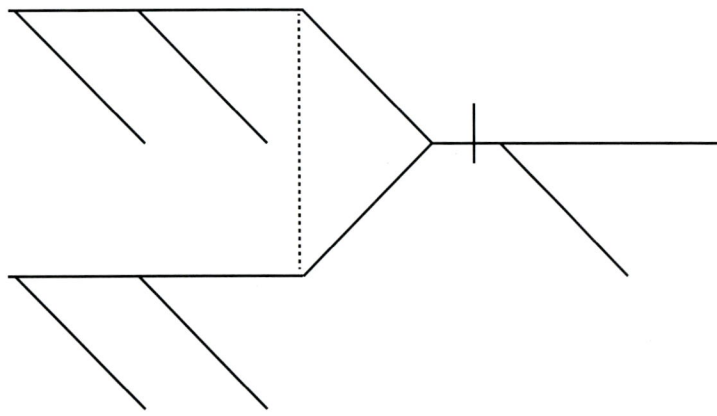

Name

6. Yellow and orange are bright colors.

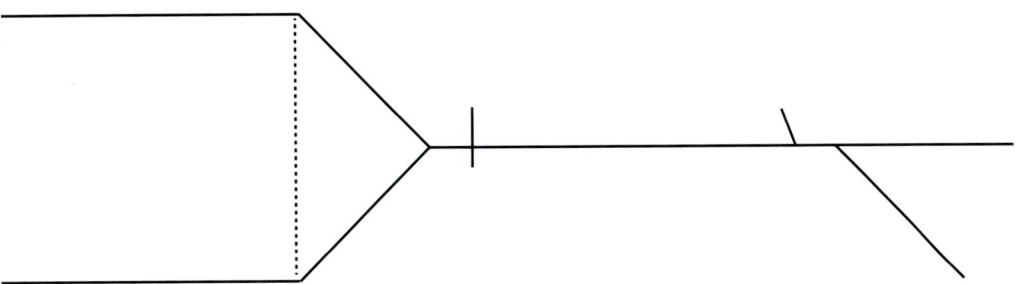

7. The hiking trails and campgrounds are well-kept.

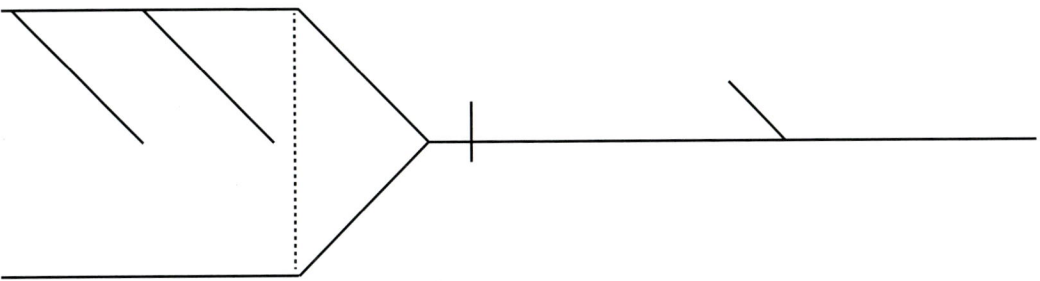

8. Jacinta and her mother sat and talked.

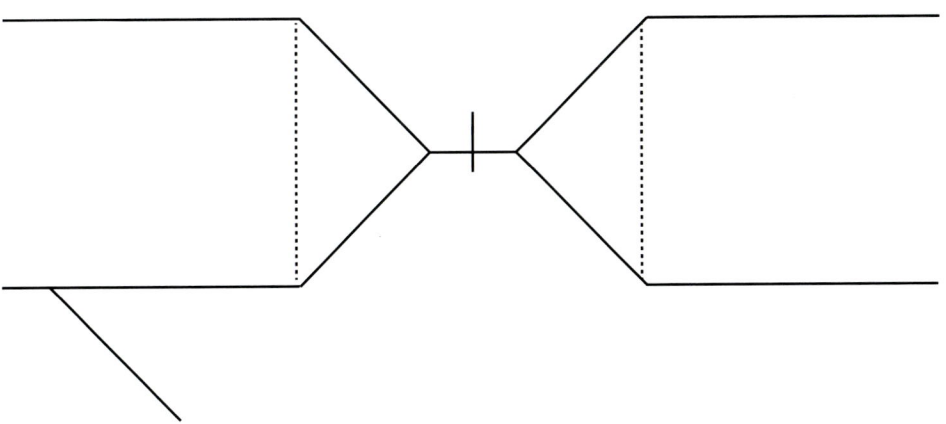

DIAGRAMMING Level 1

9. Inventors and engineers build future technology.

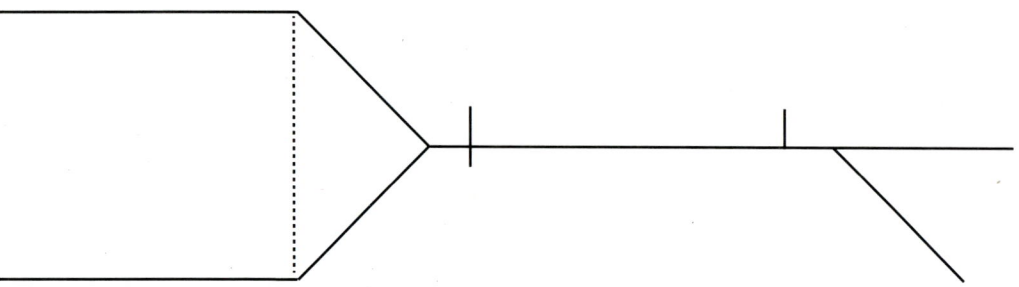

10. Kings and queens ruled.

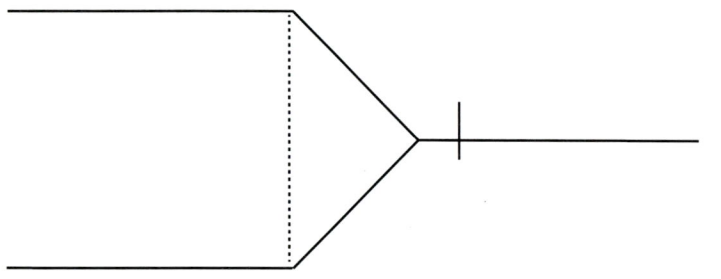

Exercise 2

Create sentences with a compound subject to fit these diagrams. Then write each one on the correct diagram.

1.

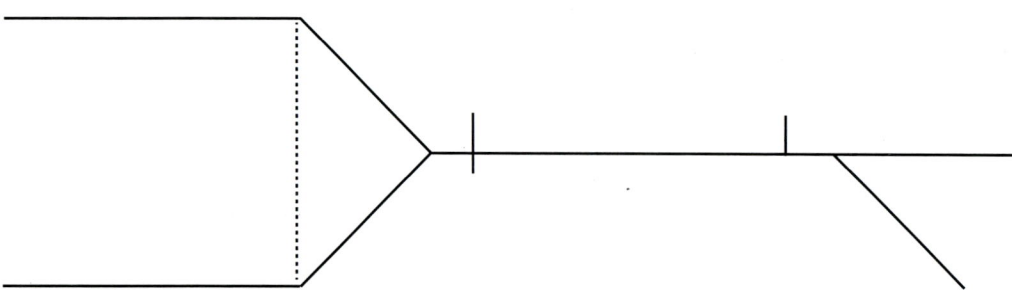

Name

DIAGRAMMING Level 1

2.

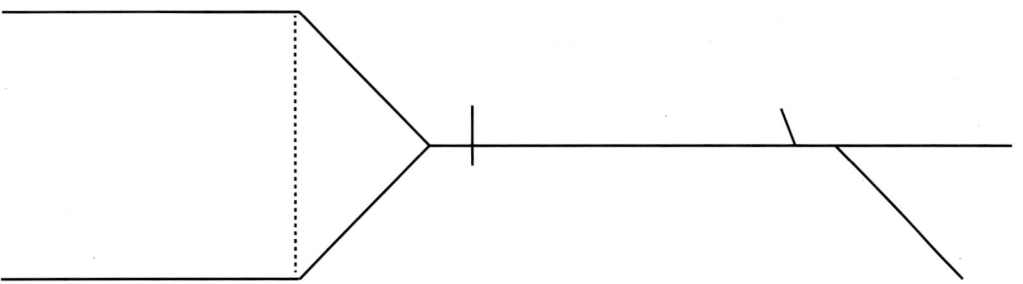

3.

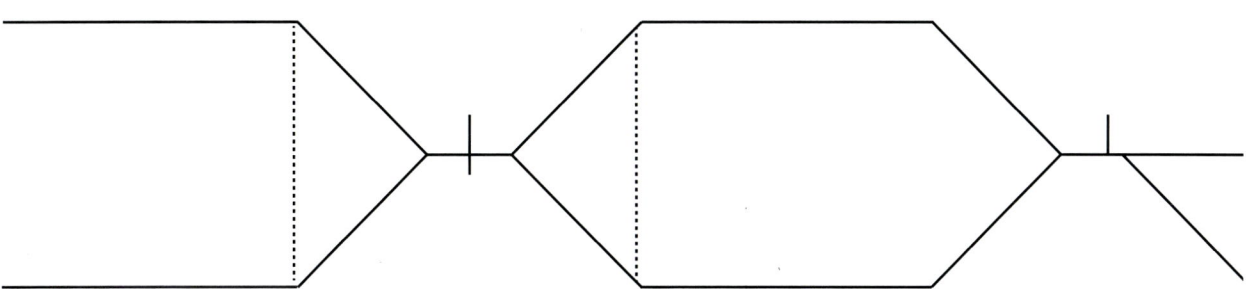

4.

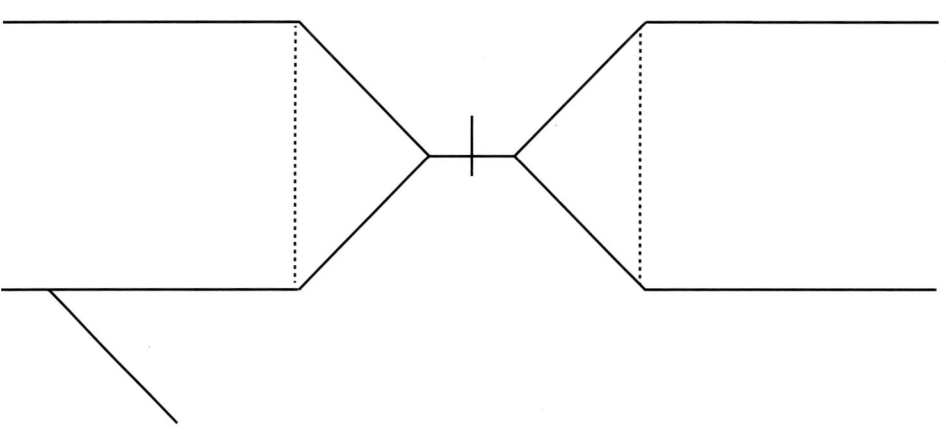

Compound Subjects 53

DIAGRAMMING Level 1

5.

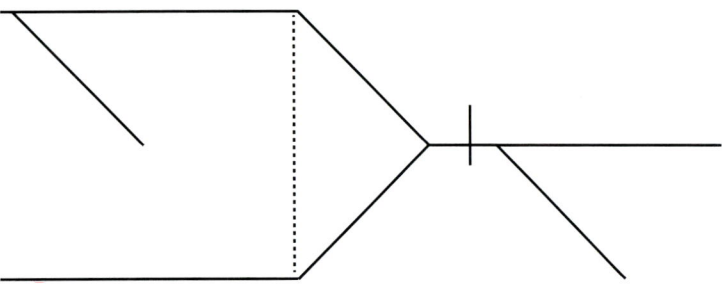

Exercise 3

Unscramble the groups of words to make complete sentences. Write the sentences on the blank lines. Then diagram them.

1. teacher the Joe disagreed and _____

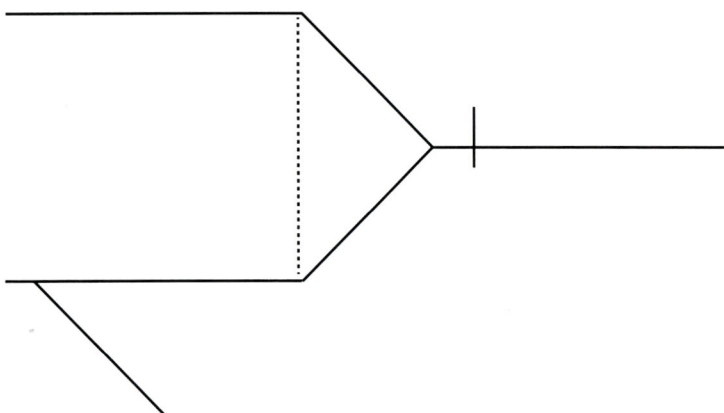

2. omelets the and cooked pancakes_____

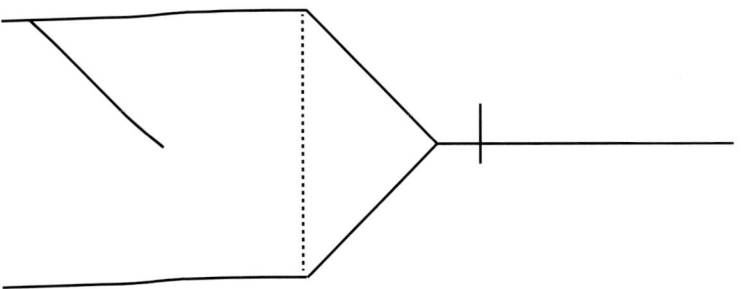

3. are Jupiter planets and Earth_____

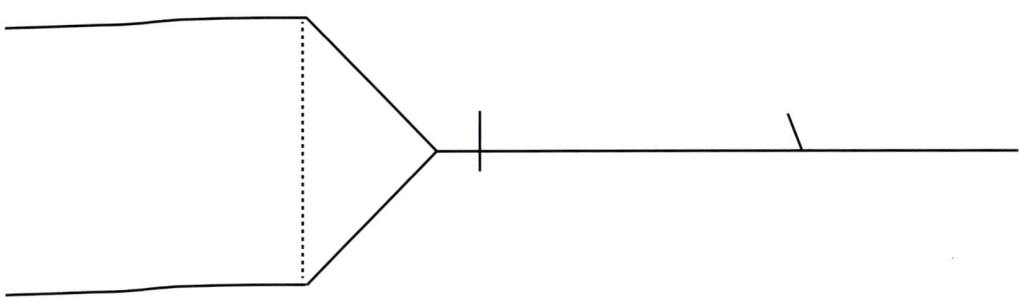

4. soccer and listened the crowd players watched and_____

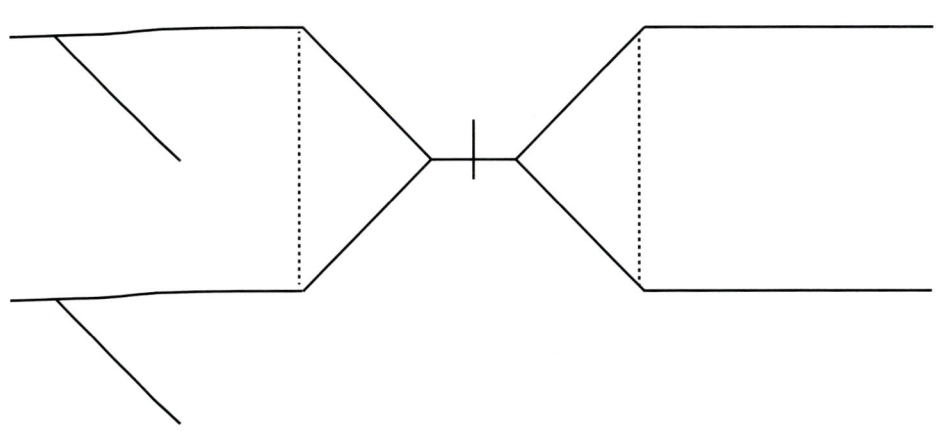

DIAGRAMMING Level 1

5. discovered and Gulliver and photographed old Peter fossils

Exercise 4

Find the mistakes in the following diagrams. Then, diagram the sentences correctly on the given, blank diagrams. Note: you may need to fix the blank diagram by drawing a new line(s).

1. The motorcycle and its brakes broke.

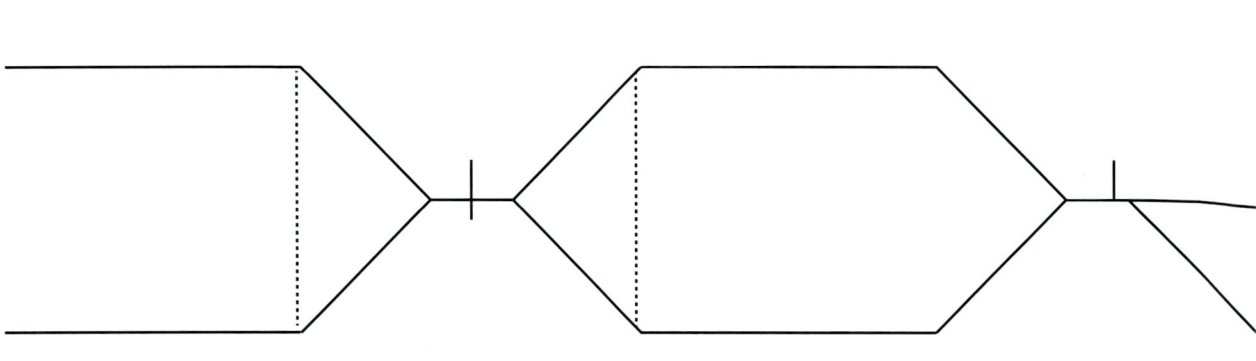

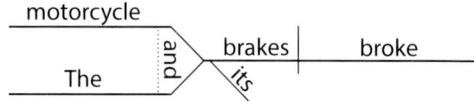

2. The village and countryside are peaceful

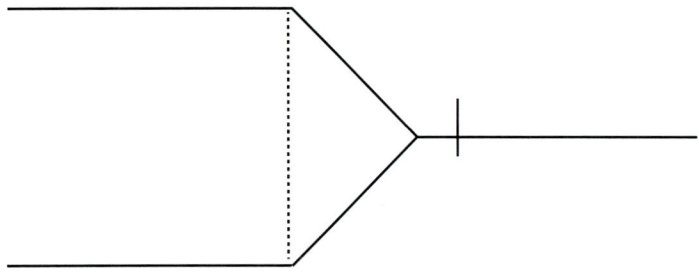

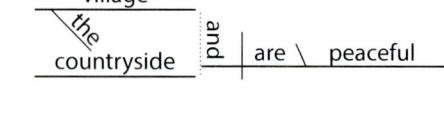

56 Compound Subjects

Name

DIAGRAMMING Level 1

3. The bishop and priests celebrated the Ordination Mass.

4. Rylan and Finnian stretched and relaxed.

5. James and John were disciples.

Compound Subjects **57**

DIAGRAMMING Level 1

COMPOUND DIRECT OBJECTS

You learned earlier that a **direct object** is a noun or pronoun in a sentence that *directly* receives the action of the **predicate**. The **direct object** answers the question *whom?* or *what?* after the action word. A **compound direct object** is when there is *more than one* **direct object** that receives the action of the **predicate**.

You diagram a **compound direct object** in the same way as a **compound predicate** except that you place the structure *after* the vertical half line (mark indicating the begining of the direct object).

I passed the quiz and the test.

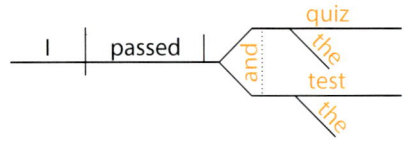

The deacon helped the priest and the parish.

Exercise 1

In the following sentences, circle the nouns, adjectives, and conjunctions that make up the compound direct object. Then diagram each sentence.

1. Nancy and Victor tossed the frisbee and football.

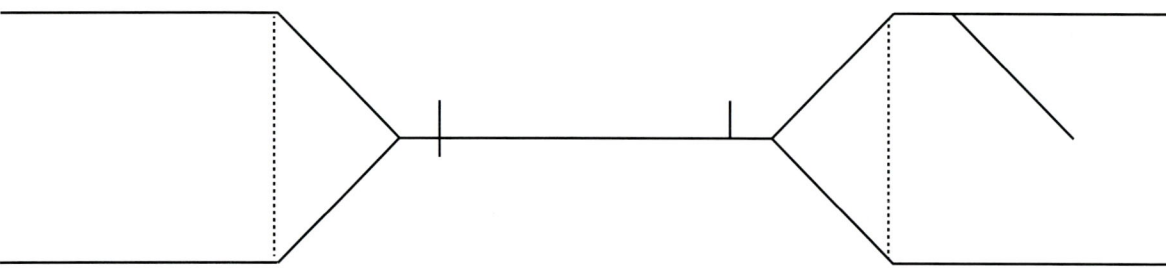

2. Great musicians write profound songs and albums.

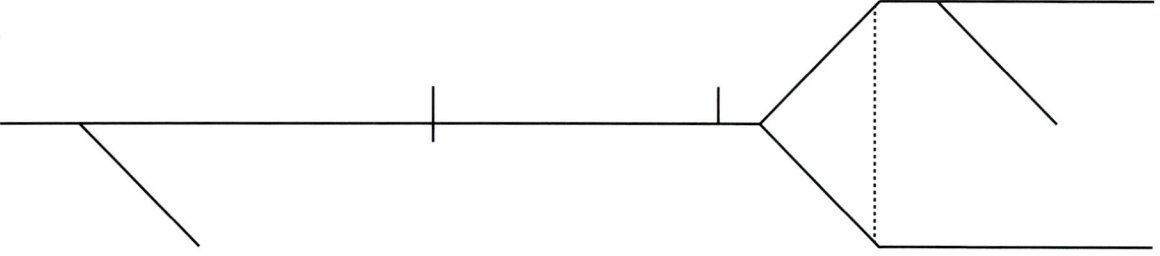

3. Bobby sent a package and a letter.

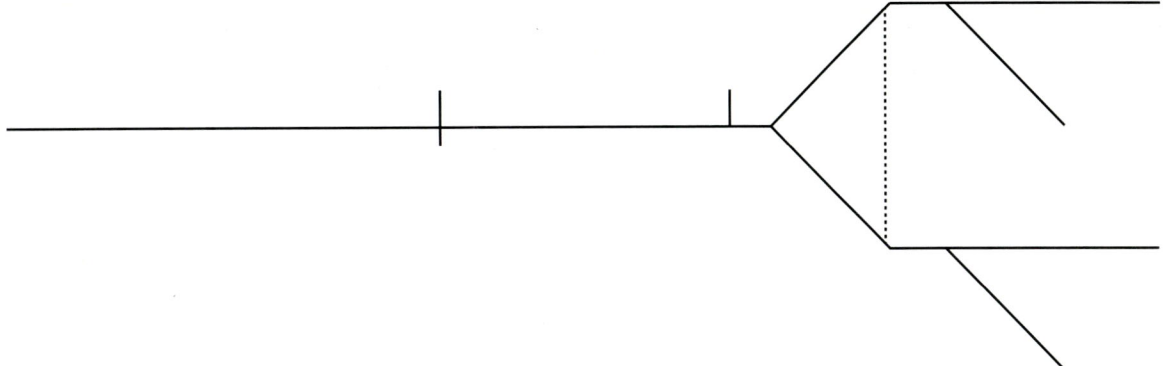

4. The President and Congress passed a new law and budget.

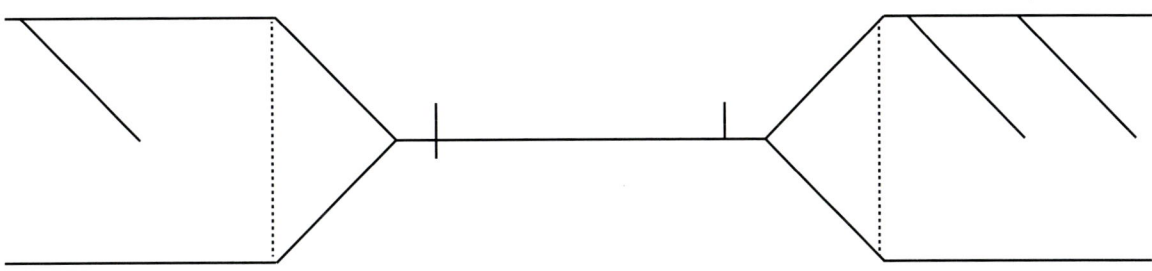

5. Julia dusted the table and the counters.

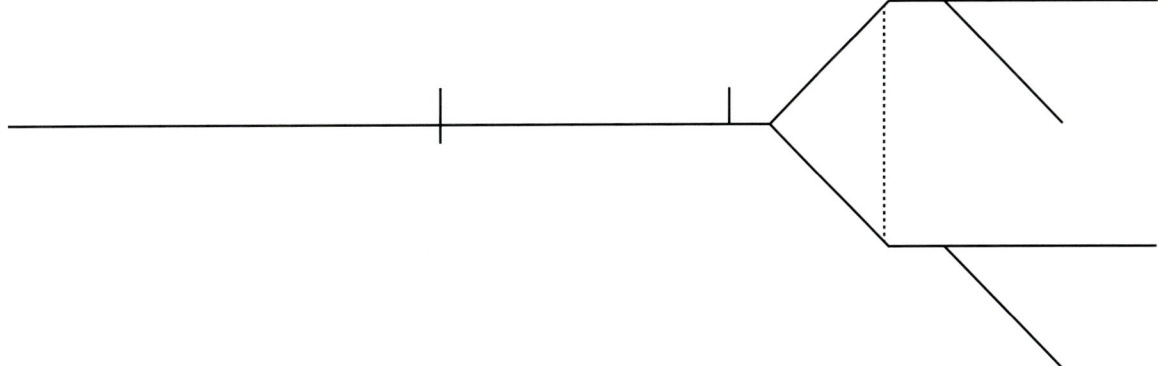

DIAGRAMMING Level 1

6. Animals form protective groups or communities.

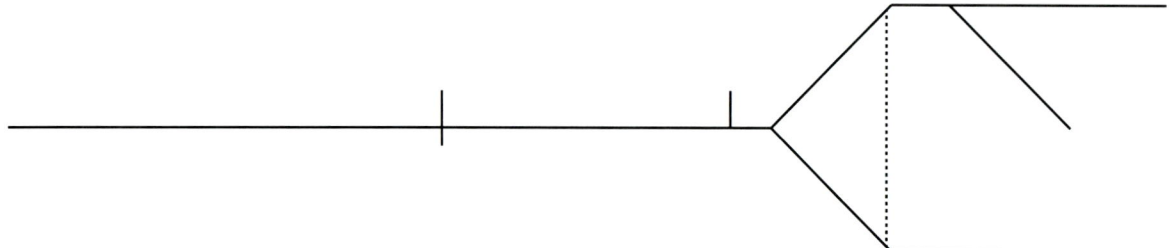

7. Freddy and Cecelia found and grabbed cups and plates.

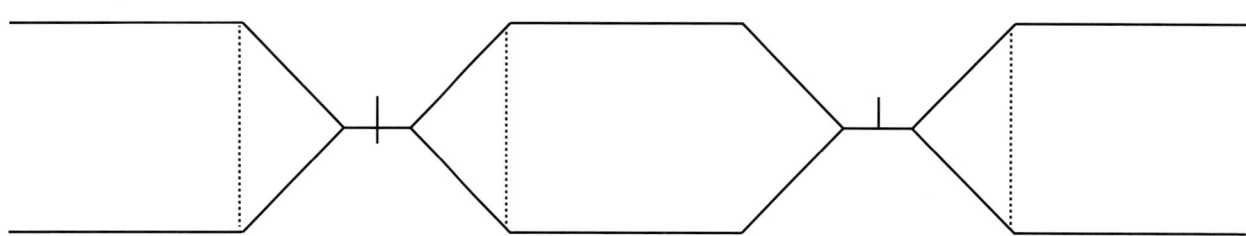

8. The Blessed Virgin brought peace and joy.

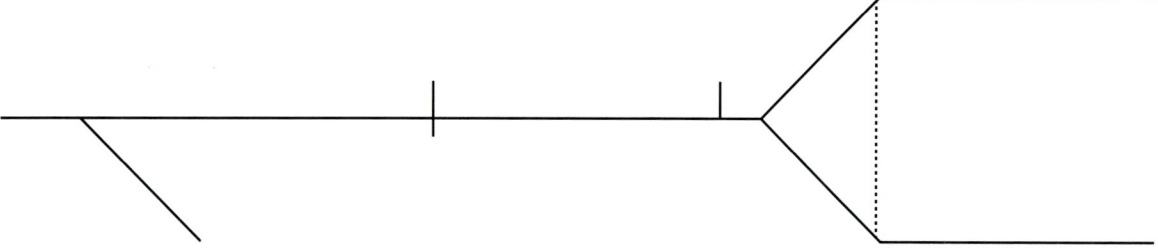

9. The sick boy ate soup and crackers.

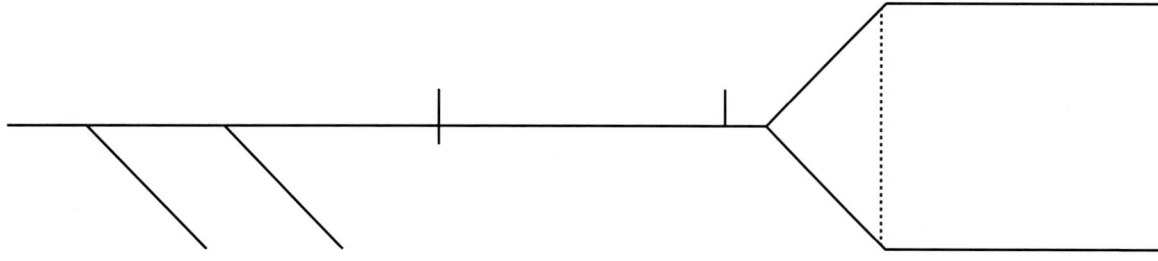

Compound Direct Objects

10. The news shocked and angered the parents and the general public.

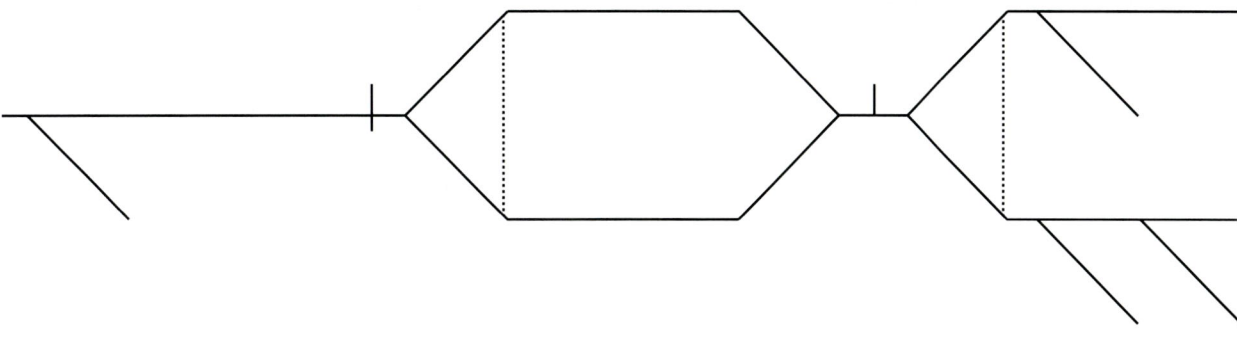

Exercise 2

Create sentences with a compound direct object to fit these diagrams. Then write each one on the correct diagram.

1.

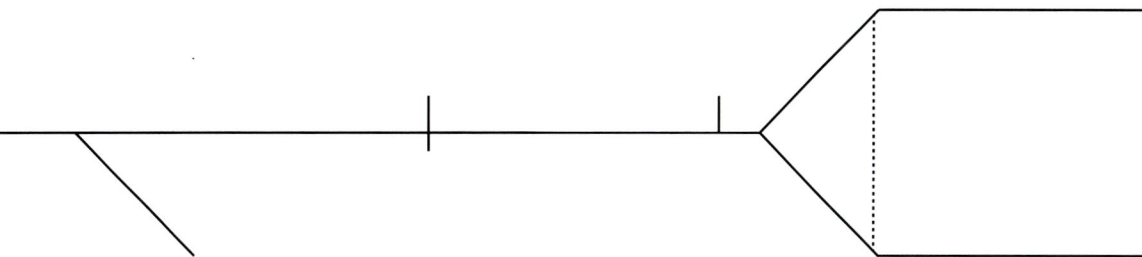

2.

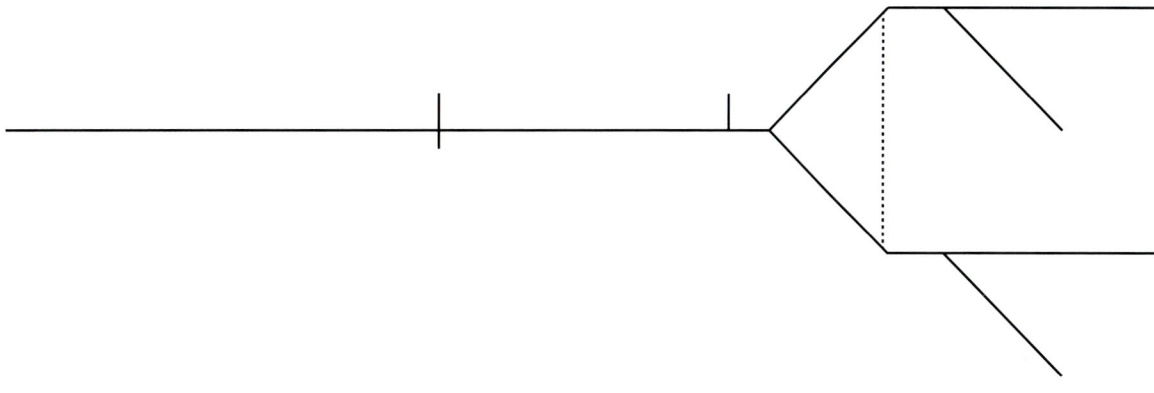

DIAGRAMMING Level 1

3.

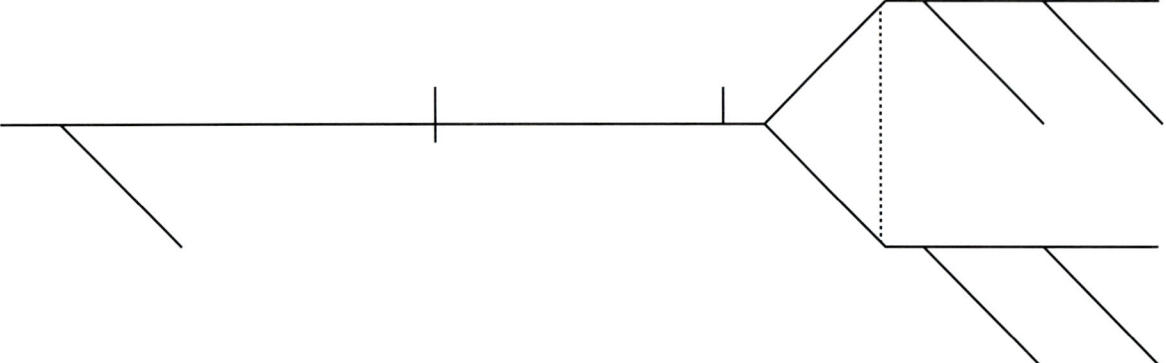

4.

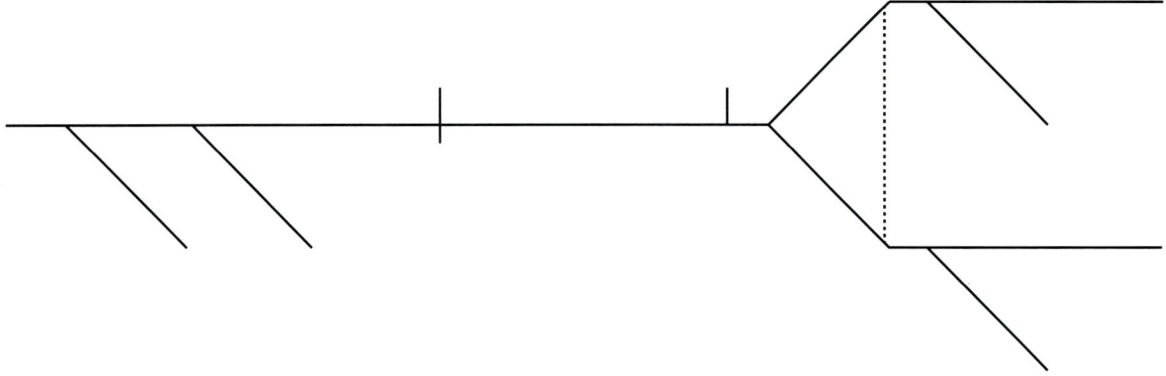

5.

Exercise 3

Unscramble the given groups of words into a complete sentence and write them on the blank provided. Then diagram them.

1. Gospel St. John a wrote letters and_____

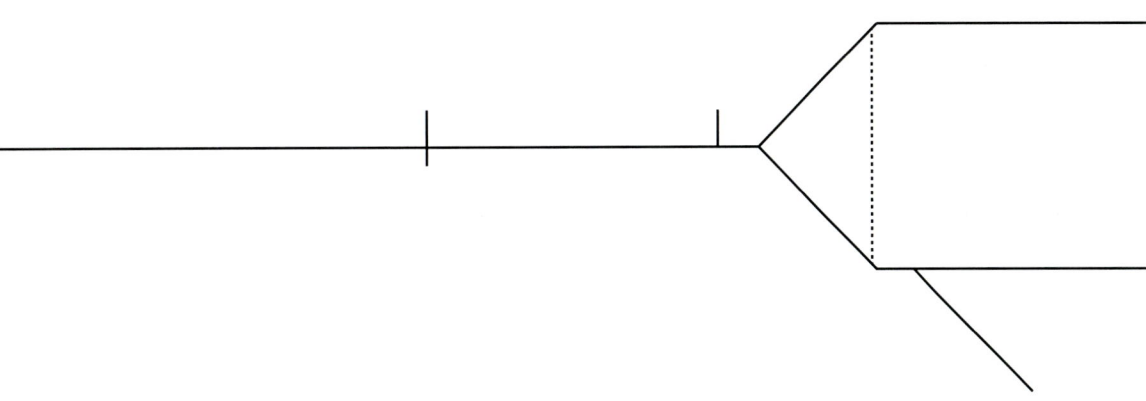

2. the noticed couple the Kelly old and grandchildren

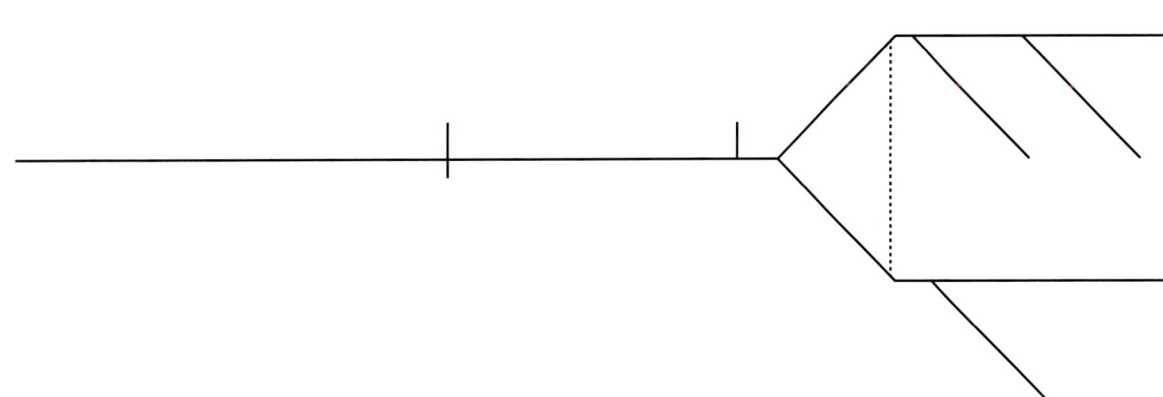

DIAGRAMMING Level 1

3. Hailey washed and the helmet the bicycle and dried

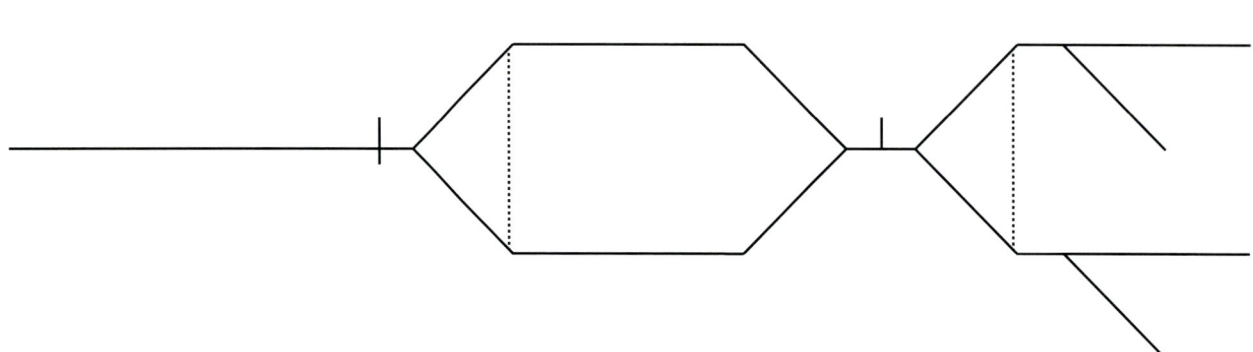

4. saved him the father and Mary's family

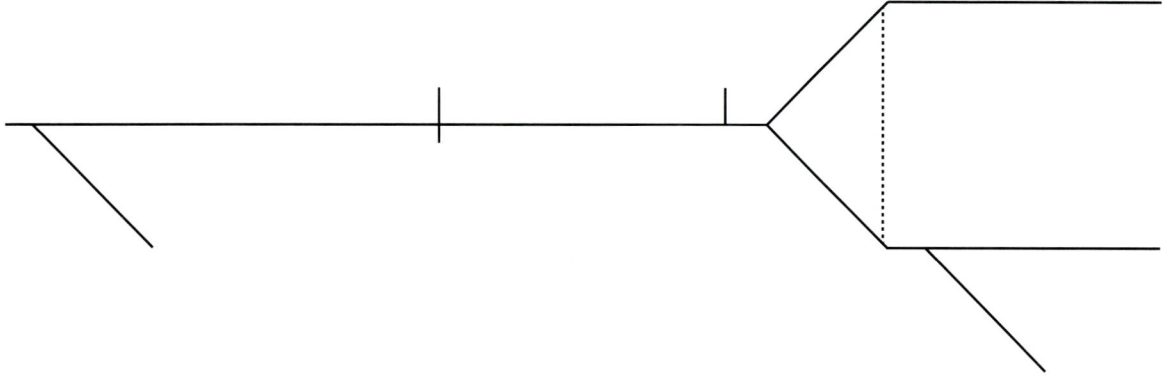

5. citizens police communities protect officers and

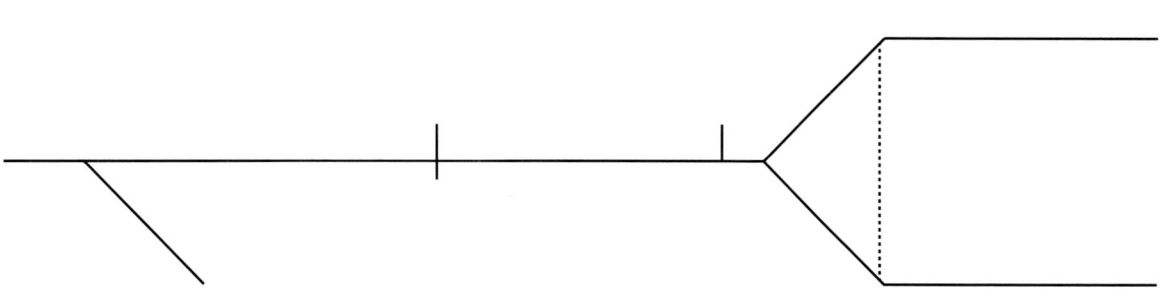

Name

DIAGRAMMING Level 1

Exercise 4

Find the mistakes in the following diagrams. Then, diagram the sentences correctly on the given, blank diagrams. Note: you may need to fix the blank diagram by drawing a new line(s).

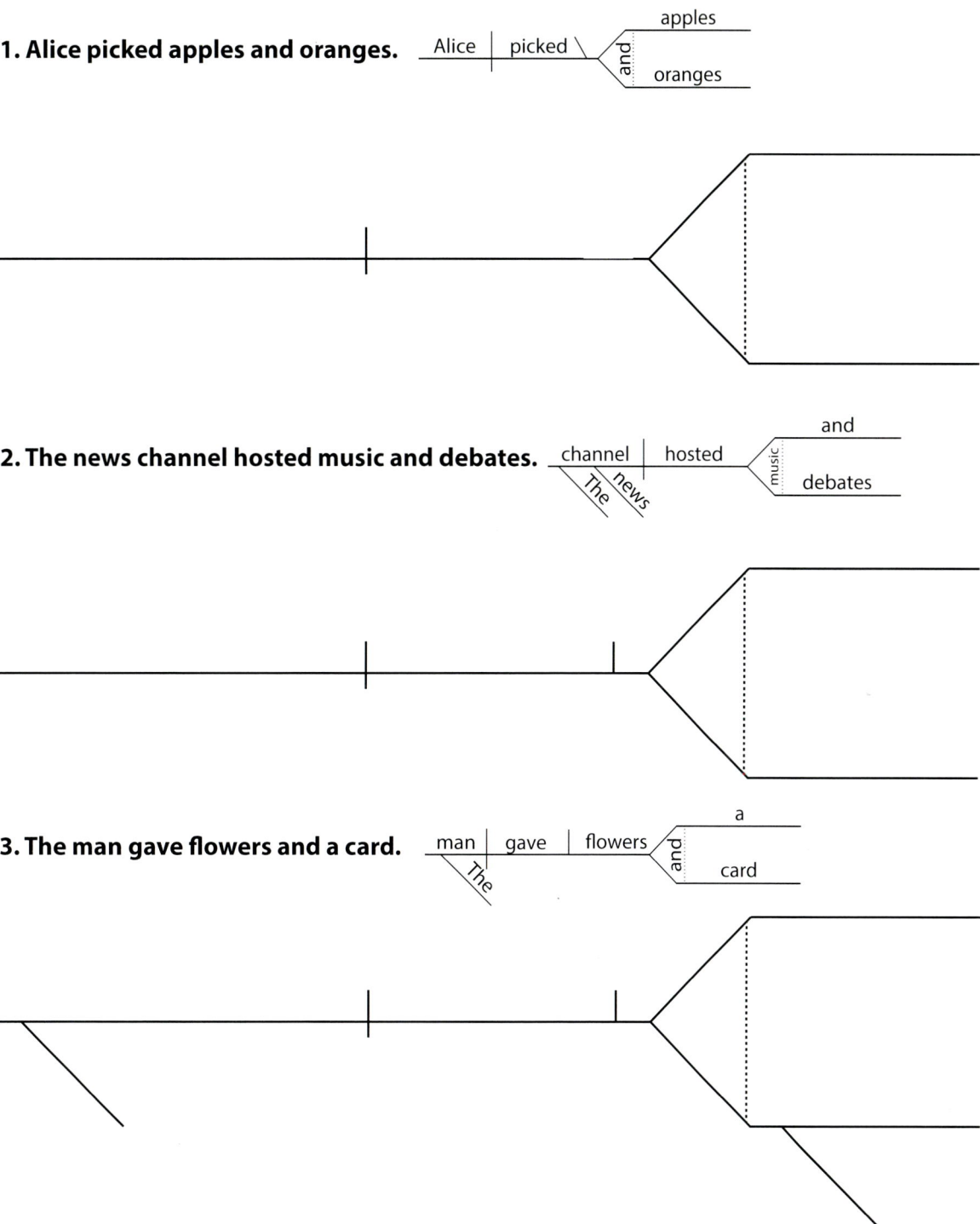

Compound Direct Objects **65**

DIAGRAMMING Level 1

4. Hannah brought cookies and pies.

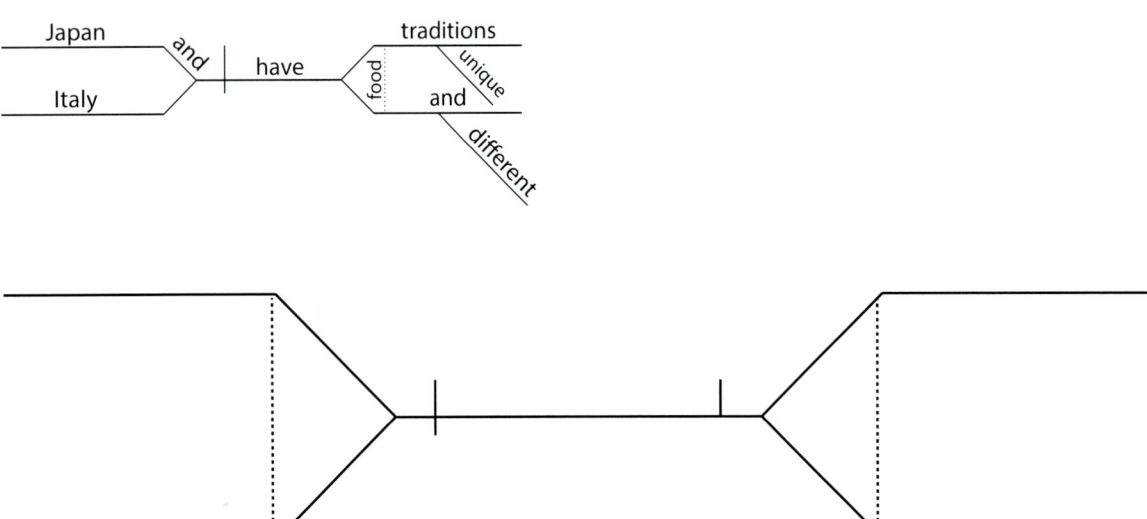

5. Japan and Italy have different food and unique traditions.

Compound Direct Objects

Name: _____

DIAGRAMMING Level 1

IMPERATIVES

Imperatives (commands) like "Stop!" or "Walk" are examples of when *you* is the **subject** even if *you* isn't expressed.

To diagram a single-word imperative sentence, place the implied *you* in parenthesis in the **subject** position and the **verb** in the **predicate** position of the diagram.

Note: Because of the simplicity of this topic, Exercises 1 and 2 are shorter.

Walk.

(you) | Walk

Stop!

(you) | Stop

Exercise 1

Diagram the following single-word sentences.

1. Stand.

2. Speak!

3. Catch!

4. Come.

Imperatives 67

DIAGRAMMING Level 1

5. Jump!

Exercise 2

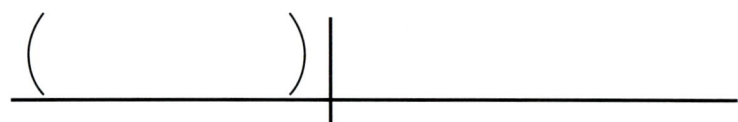

Create single-word command sentences to fit the blank diagrams.

1.
2.

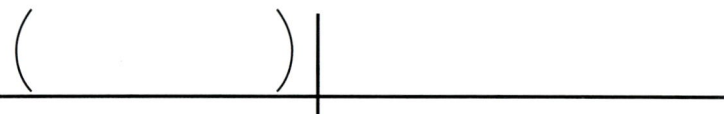

Name

DIAGRAMMING Level 1

REVIEW: DIRECT OBJECTS

Review Exercise 1

In the following sentences, circle the predicate, underline the subject once and the direct object twice. Then diagram each sentence.

1. Christ forgives sins.

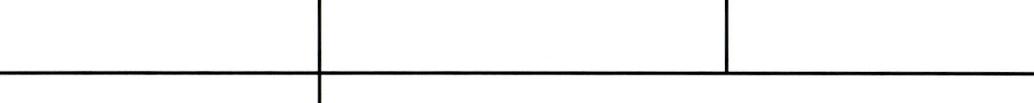

2. The cat bit the toy.

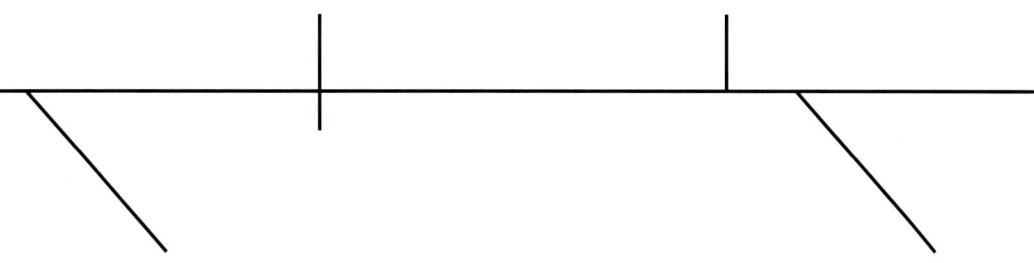

3. Gerald taught the class.

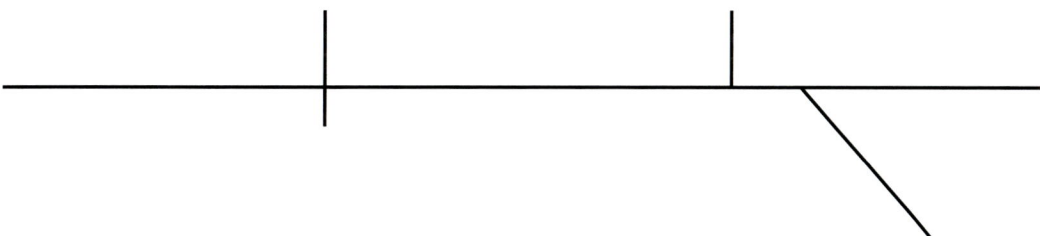

4. The waves smashed the beach.

Review 69

DIAGRAMMING Level 1

5. The nomad packed a tent.

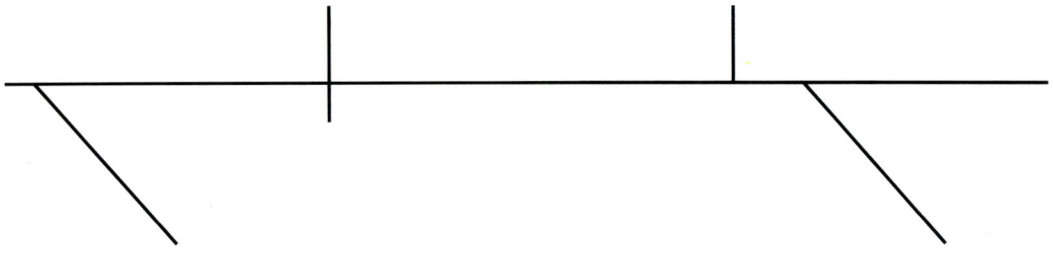

Review Exercise 2

Create sentences with a direct object to fit these diagrams. Then write each one on the correct diagram.

1.

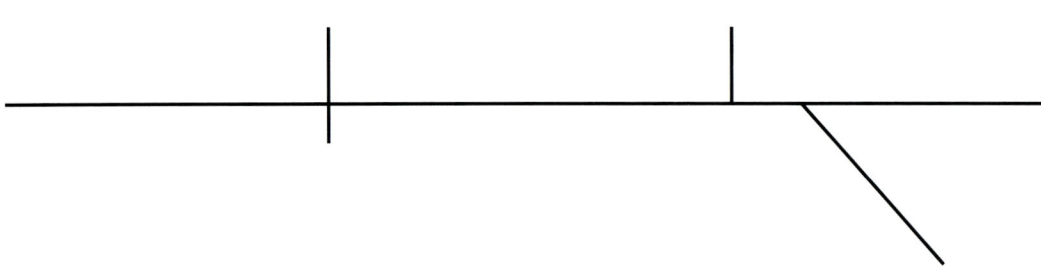

2.

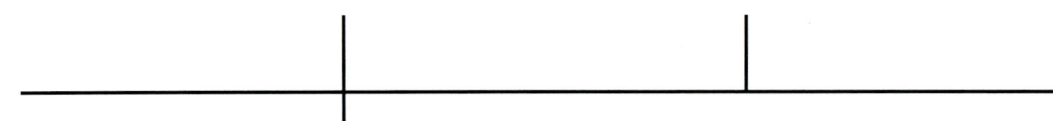

REVIEW: ADJECTIVES

Review Exercise 1

In the following sentences, underline the adjectives once and circle the nouns they modify. Then diagram each sentence.

1. This train rumbled.

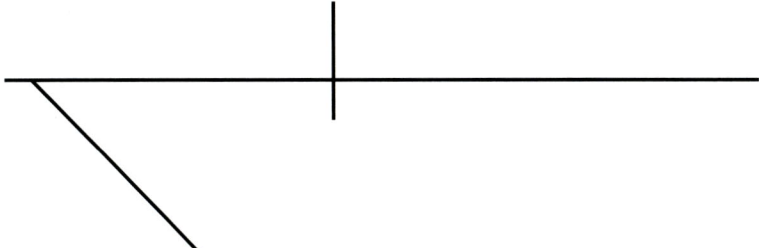

2. The older cousin called.

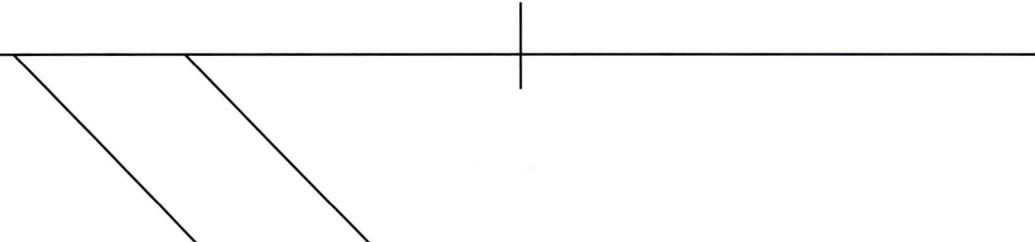

3. Strong storms will arrive.

4. He cooks Mexican food.

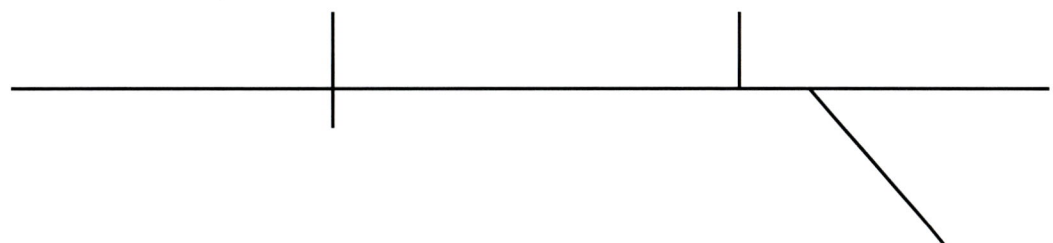

DIAGRAMMING Level 1

5. Clarissa bought a new dress.

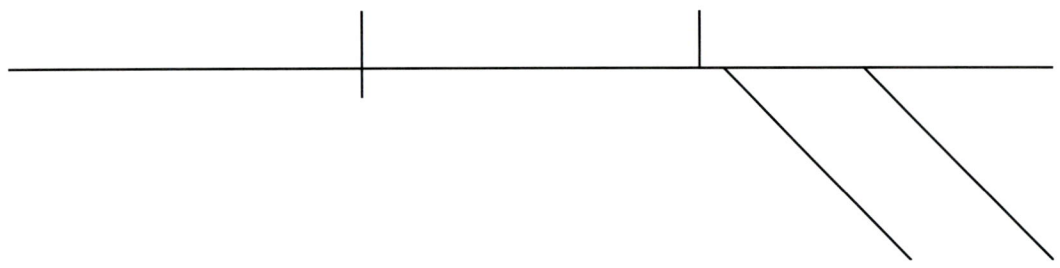

Review Exercise 2
Create sentences to fit these diagrams. Then write each one on the correct diagram.

1.

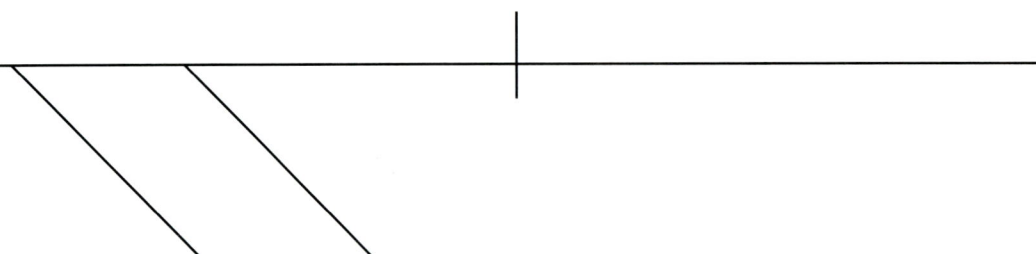

2.

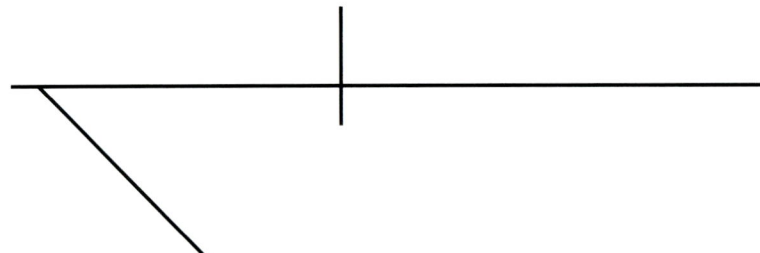

Name

DIAGRAMMING Level 1

REVIEW: SUBJECTIVE COMPLEMENTS

Review Exercise 1

In the following sentences, underline the subjective complements once and circle the nouns they complement. Then diagram each sentence.

1. A ski vacation can be pleasant.

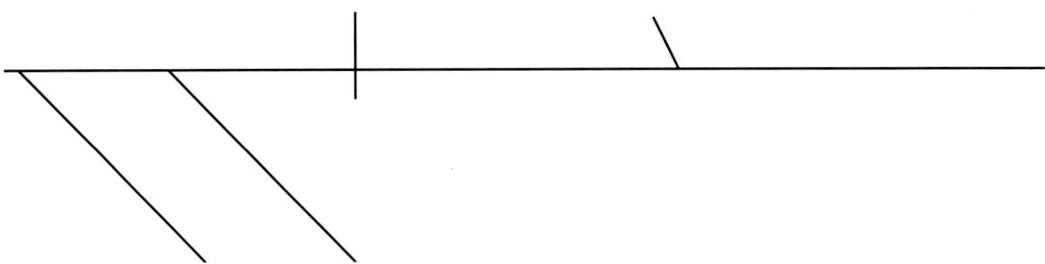

2. Father Michael is a good priest.

3. Mothers are resilient.

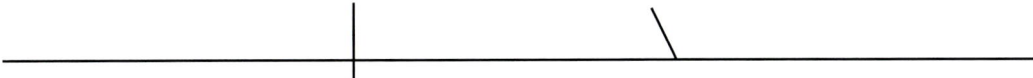

4. The woman will be a nurse.

Review 73

DIAGRAMMING Level 1

5. This store is huge.

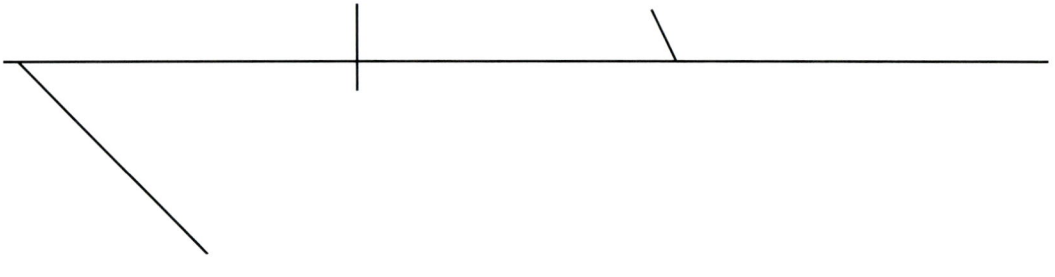

Review Exercise 2

Create sentences with a subjective complement to fit these diagrams. Then write each one on the correct diagram.

1.

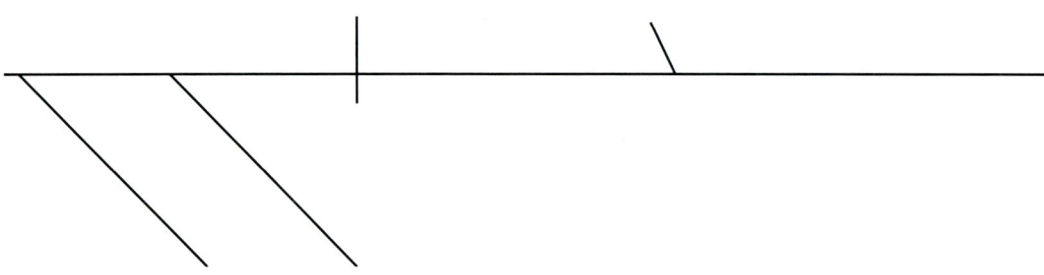

2.

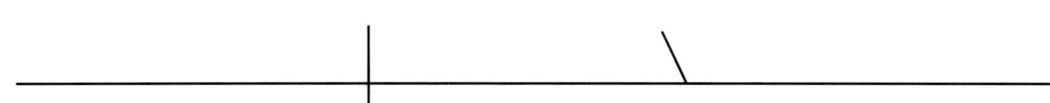

Name _____

DIAGRAMMING Level 1

REVIEW: ADVERBS (TIME, PLACE, AND MANNER)

Review Exercise 1

In the following sentences, underline the adverbs once and circle the predicates they modify. Then diagram each sentence.

1. Xavier awoke early.

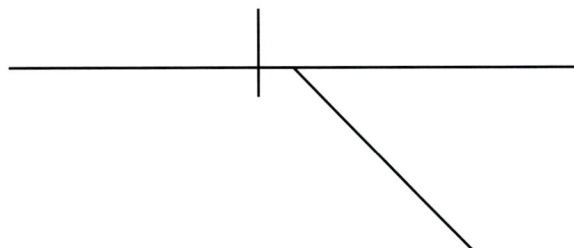

2. The electrician struggled nearby.

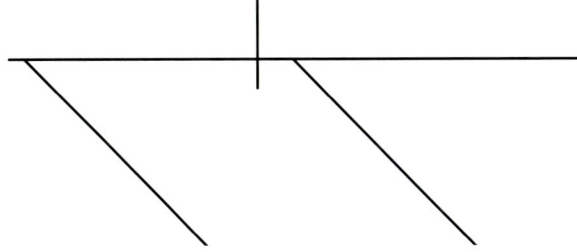

3. Sandra beautifully finished the dress.

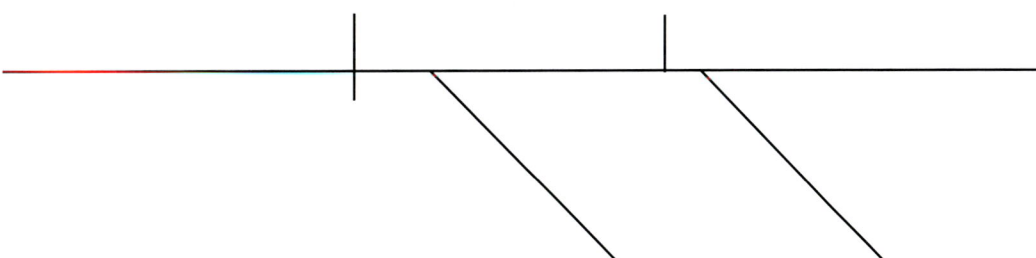

4. Unhappy babies can cry loudly.

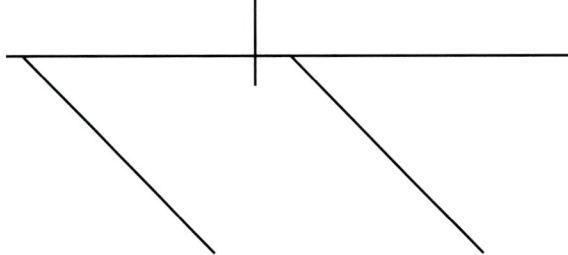

DIAGRAMMING Level 1

5. He still climbs.

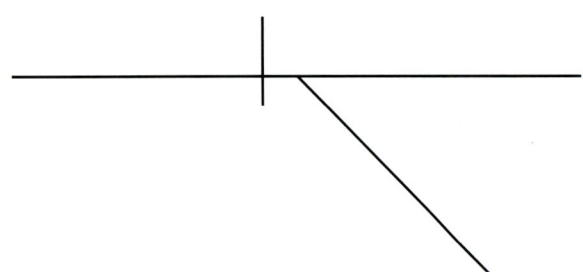

Review Exercise 2

Create sentences with an adverb to fit these diagrams. Then write each one on the correct diagram.

1.

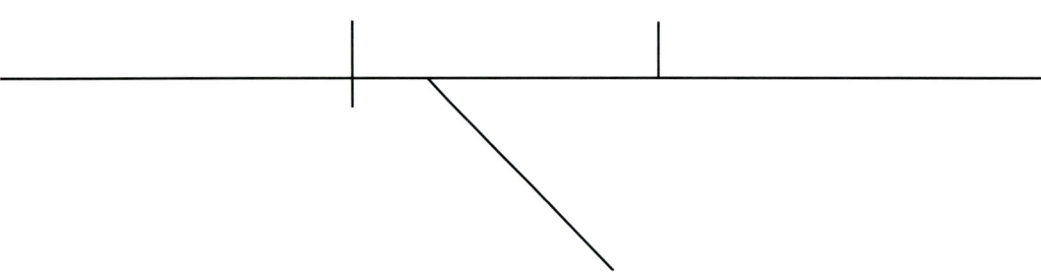

2.

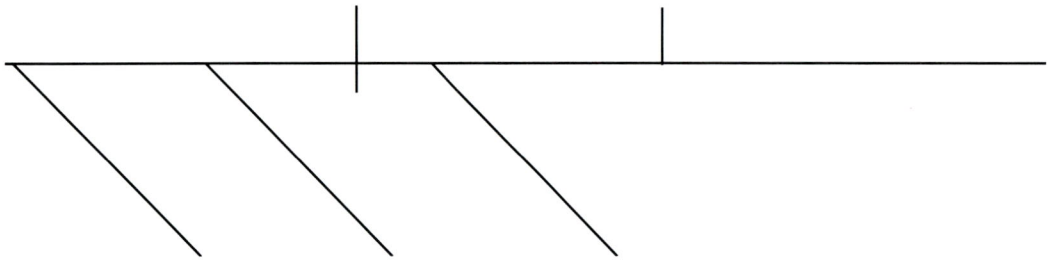

Name _____

DIAGRAMMING Level 1

REVIEW: COMPOUND PREDICATES

Review Exercise 1

In the following sentences, circle the verbs and conjunctions that make up the compound predicate. Then diagram each sentence.

1. Matthew reads and writes.

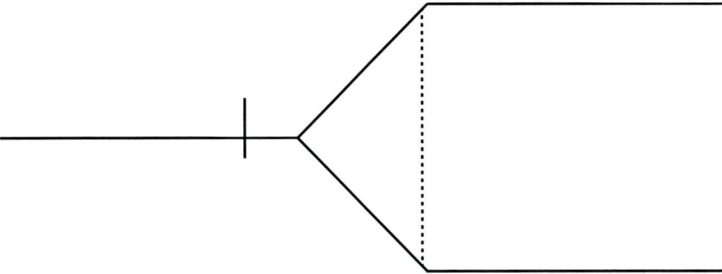

2. The car swerved and braked.

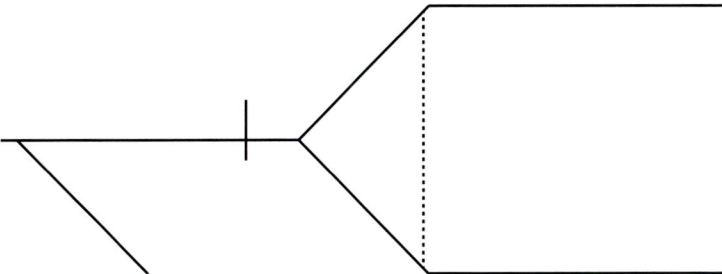

3. Nick proofreads and edits the papers.

Review 77

DIAGRAMMING Level 1

4. A northern wind howled and blew.

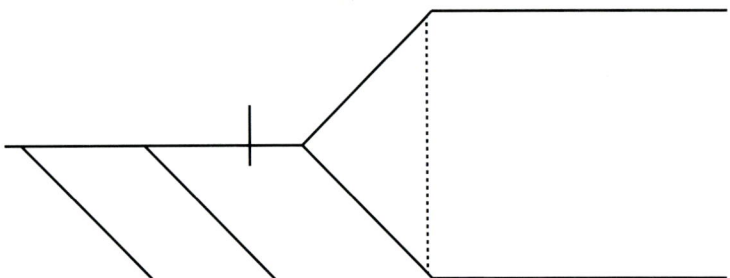

5. The famous photographer took and sent stunning photos.

Review Exercise 2

Create sentences with a compound predicate to fit these diagrams. Then write each one on the correct diagram.

1.

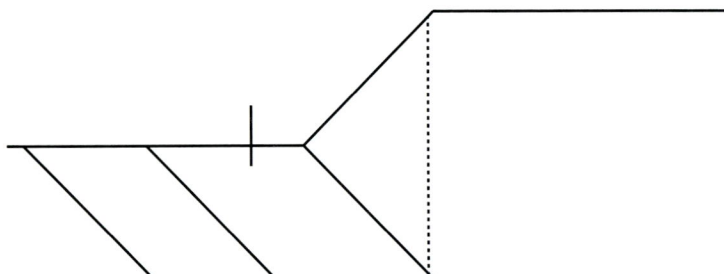

2.

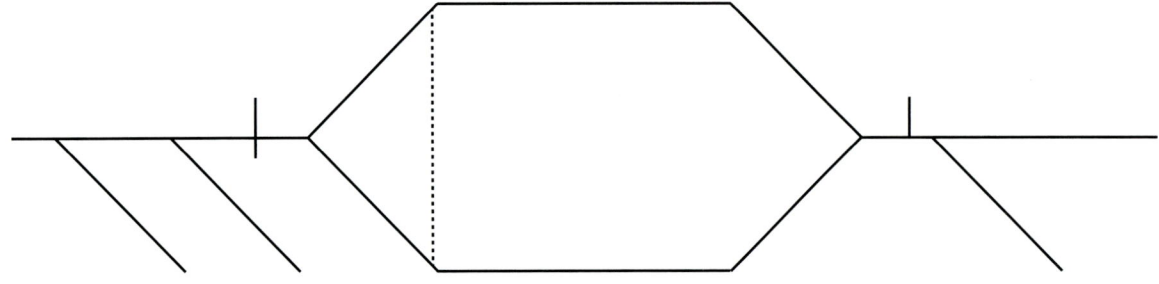

Name

DIAGRAMMING Level 1

REVIEW: COMPOUND SUBJECTS

Review Exercise 1

In the following sentences, circle the nouns, pronouns, adjectives, and conjunctions in the compound subject. Then diagram each sentence.

1. The abbot and the prior received the postulants.

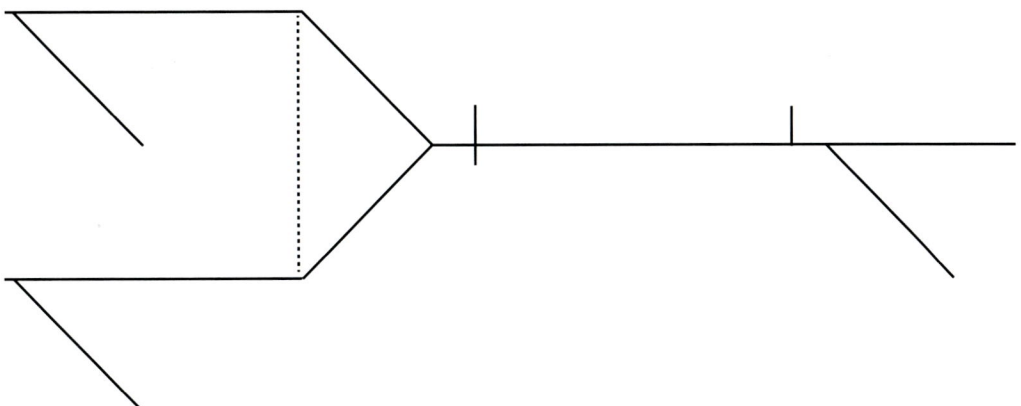

2. Rick and Joanna calculated and determined the budget.

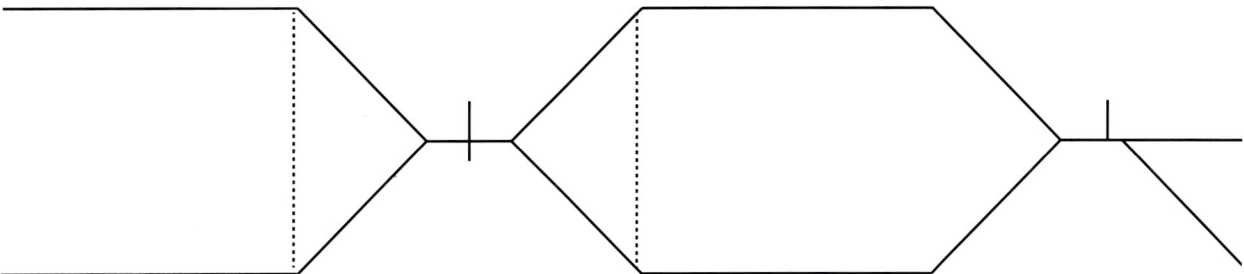

3. Abraham and Sarah soon departed.

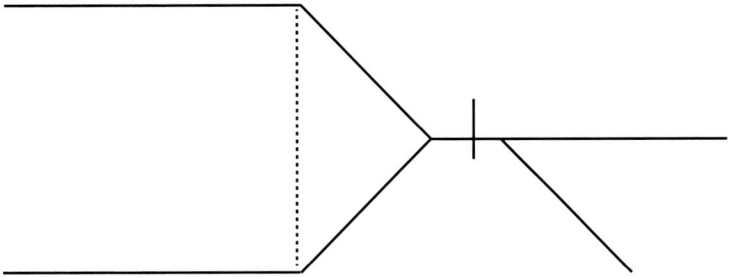

Review 79

DIAGRAMMING Level 1

4. My friends and I meet frequently.

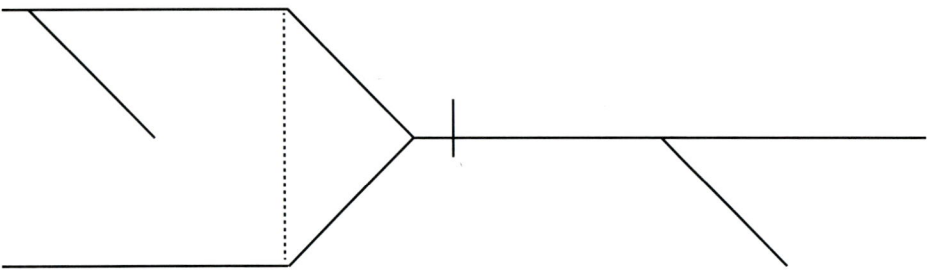

5. Math and science can be difficult subjects.

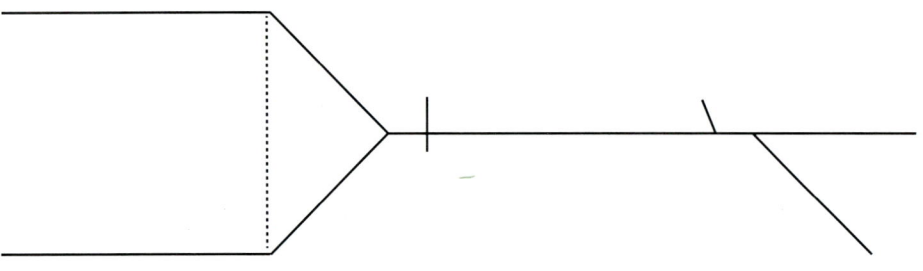

Review Exercise 2

Create sentences with a compound subject to fit these diagrams. Then write each one on the correct diagram.

1.

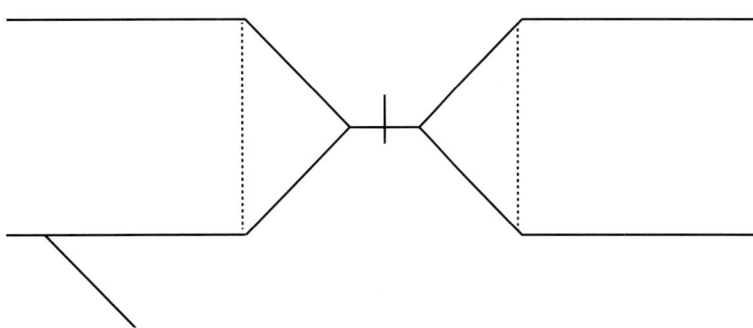

2.

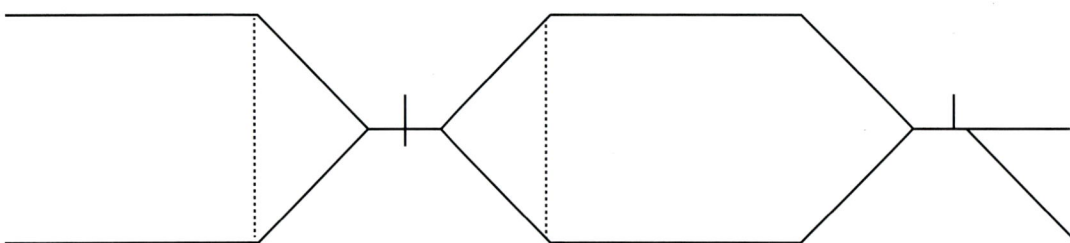

Name

REVIEW: COMPOUND DIRECT OBJECTS

Review Exercise 1

In the following sentences, circle the nouns, conjunctions and adjectives that form the compound direct object. Then diagram each sentence.

1. My grandfather hopefully will enjoy a vacation and a new car.

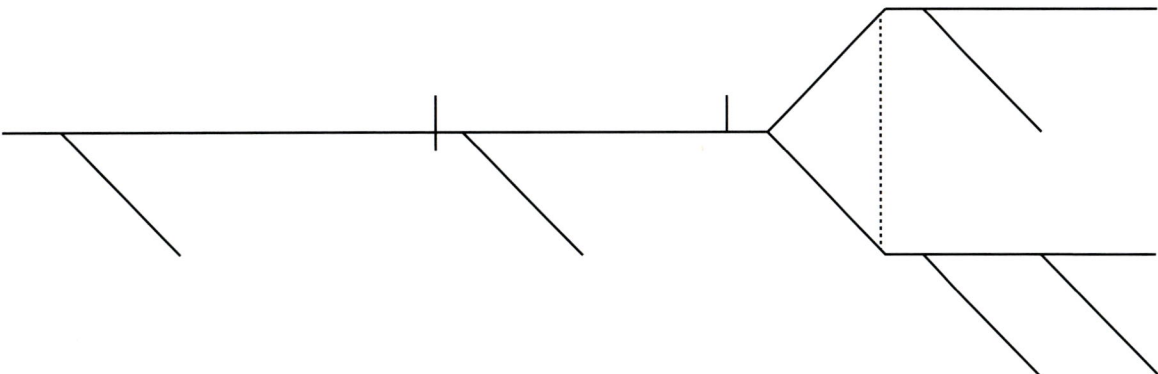

2. The snake crossed the river and the road.

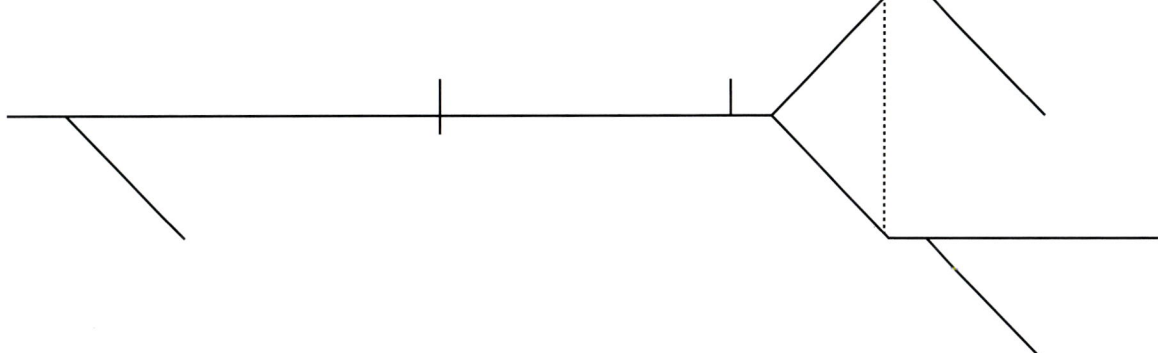

3. Shannon used the brush and the comb.

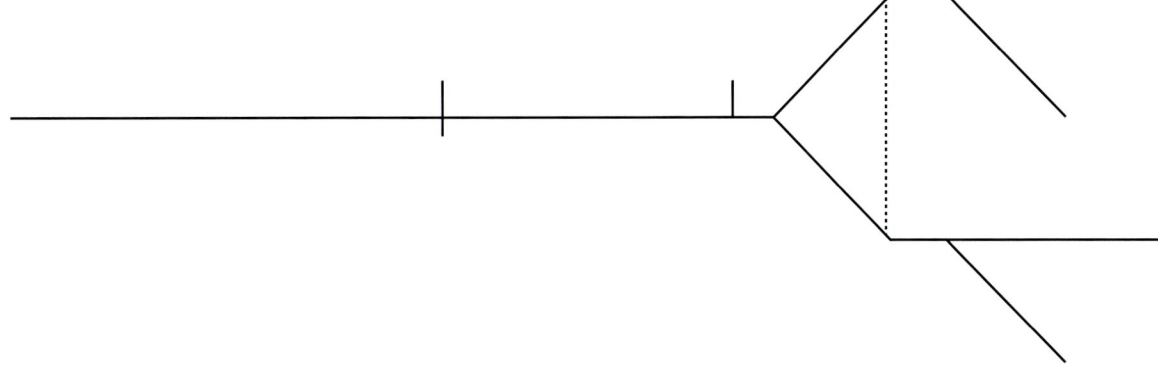

DIAGRAMMING Level 1

4. Growing towns and cities will create great jobs and communities.

5. Mr. Holmes planted squash and peas.

Review Exercise 2

Create sentences with a compound direct object to fit these diagrams. Then write each one on the correct diagram.

1.

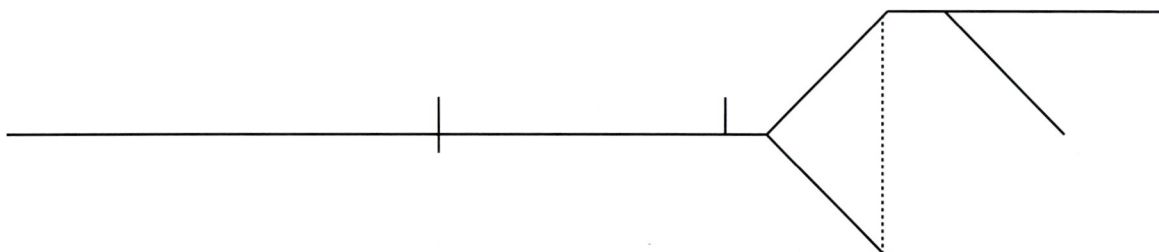

2.

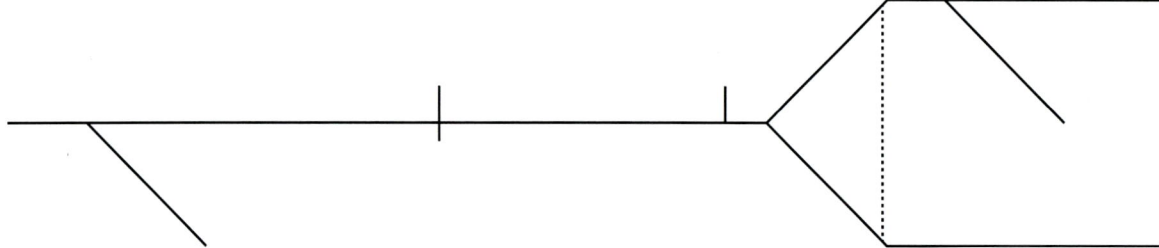

ANSWER KEY

Subject/Predicate-Exercise 1
1. Cats jump.

    cats | jump

2. The truck starts.

    truck | starts
    The

3. Dogs bark.

    Dogs | bark

4. The boy yelled.

    boy | yelled
    The

5. Sharks swim.

    Sharks | swim

6. The leaves fell.

    leaves | fell
    The

7. A bird dives.

    bird | dives
    A

8. Girls laugh.

    Girls | laugh

9. Airplanes fly.

    Airplanes | fly

10. A mouse scurried.

    mouse | scurried
    A

Subject/Predicate-Exercise 3
1. The baker baked.

    baker | baked
    The

2. He believes.

    He | believes

3. An artist creates.

    artist | creates
    An

4. Ballerinas dance.

    Ballerinas | dance

5. The student writes.

    student | writes
    The

Subject/Predicate Exercise 4
1. hat | fell
   The

2. man | studied
   The

3. Bees | sting

4. child | hides
   A

5. phone | rang
   The

Answer Key 83

Direct Objects- Exercise 1
1. (She) read the newspaper.

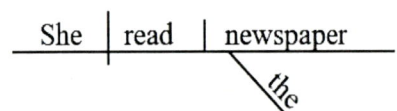

2. (Juan) wrote letters.

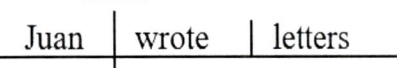

3. The (wind) rips the sails.

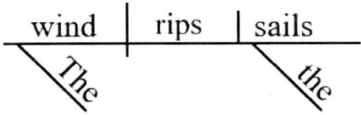

4. (God) saved her.

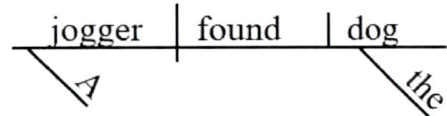

5. (Fire) burns wood.

Fire | burns | wood

6. (Margaret) splashed Mark.

Margaret | splashed | Mark

7. A (jogger) found the dog.

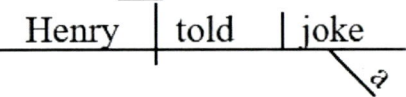

8. (Henry) told a joke.

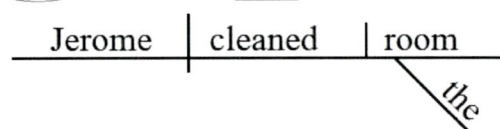

9. (Jerome) cleaned the room.

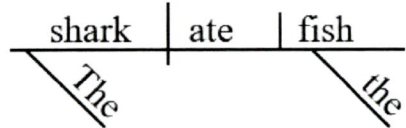

10. The (shark) ate the fish.

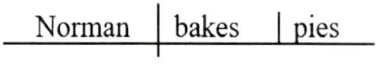

Direct Object- Exercise 3
1. Norman bakes pies.

Norman | bakes | pies

2. Elizabeth found him.

Elizabeth | found | him

3. The dog chewed the bone.

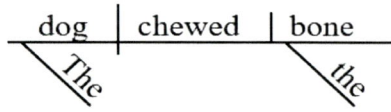

4. Students read books.

Students | read | books

5. I answered the question.

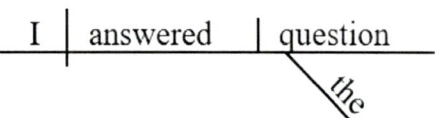

Direct Object-Exercise 4
1.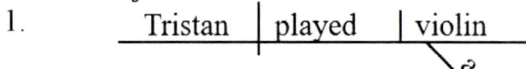
2. Priests | celebrate | Mass
3.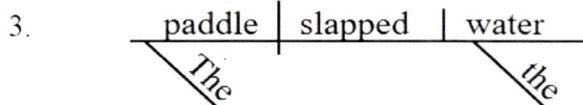
4. Horses | eat | oats
5.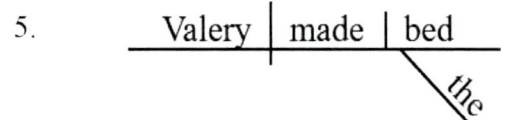

Adjectives- Exercise 1
1. The large balloon floated.

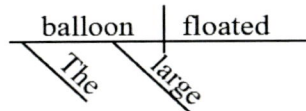

2. The French knight left the palace.

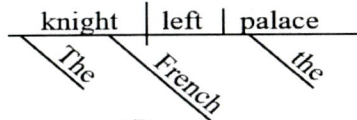

3. That prized horse won the race.

4. A beautiful flower bloomed.

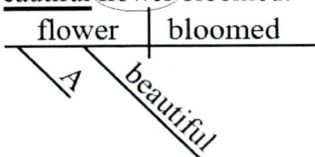

5. The successful doctor spoke.

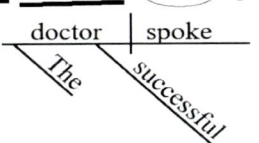

6. Tom's ship sailed the Atlantic coastline.

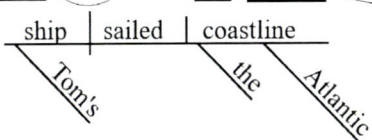

7. The expensive glove disappeared.

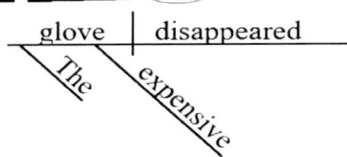

8. The kind uncle arrived.

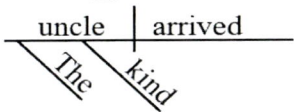

9. A lightning bolt split a tree.

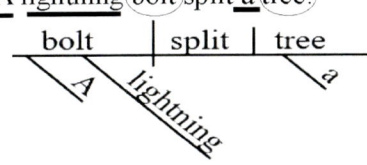

10. Angry politicians argue.

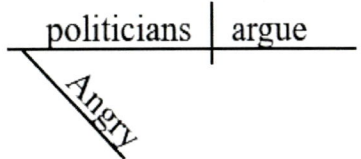

Adjectives- Exercise 3
1. The police officer negotiated.

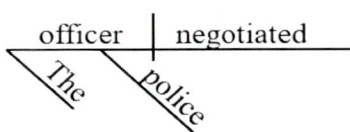

2. The skillful actor performed a monologue. – OR – A skillful actor performed the monologue.

'A' and 'The' are interchangeable

3. The red truck rumbled.

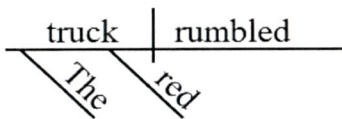

4. Jesus healed the sick man.

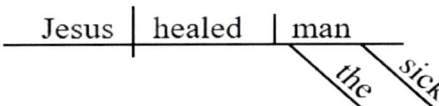

5. The tennis matches continued.

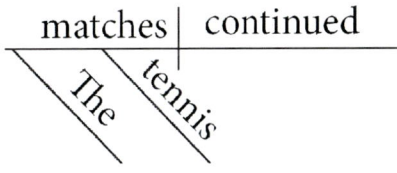

Answer Key 85

Adjectives-Exercise 4
1.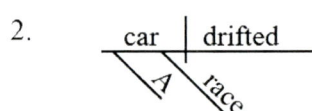
2.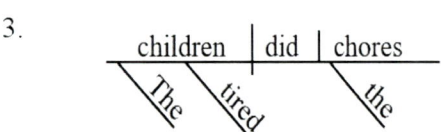
3.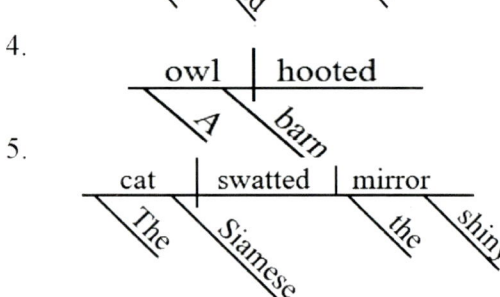
4.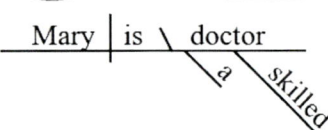
5.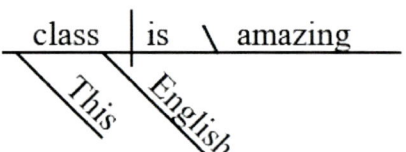

Subjective Complements- Exercise 1
1. Mary is a skilled doctor.
   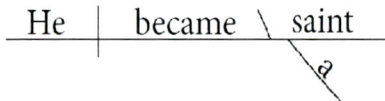
2. This English class is amazing.
   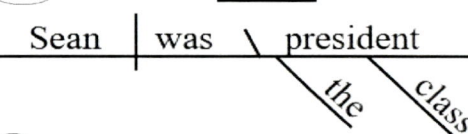
3. He became a saint.
   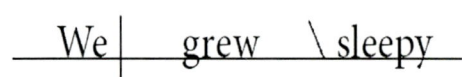
4. Sean was the class president.

   Sean | was \ president
               the \ class

5. We grew sleepy.

   We | grew \ sleepy

6. The dog was a puppy.
   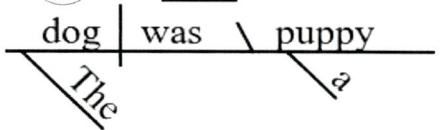
7. The beach is crowded.
   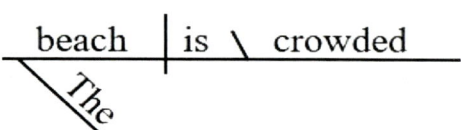
8. It is she.
   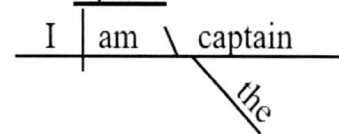
9. I am the captain.
   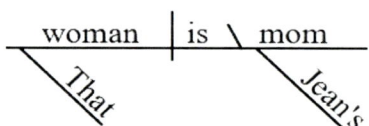
10. That woman is Jean's mom.

    woman | is \ mom
    That   Jean's

Subjective Complements- Exercise 3
1. Nathan is a college student.
   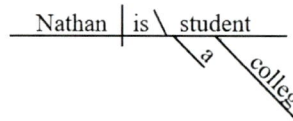
2. Classical instruments are expensive.
   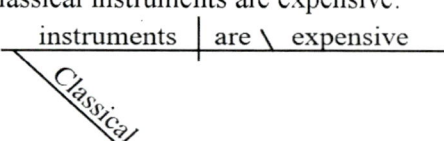
3. St. George was English.

   St George | was \ English

4. A good movie is entertaining.
   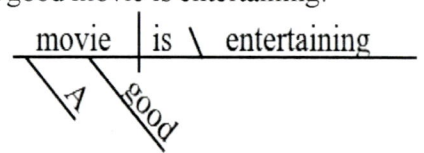
5. This man was a lawyer.
   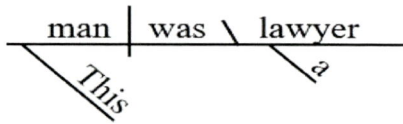

Subjective Complements- Exercise 4
1. Veronica is \ dancer

   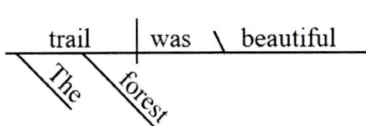

2.

   trail was \ beautiful

   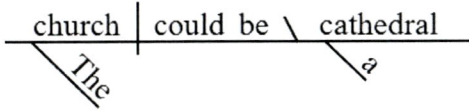

3. swans were \ old

4. Gene is \ poet

5. Pope St John Paul II was \ man

   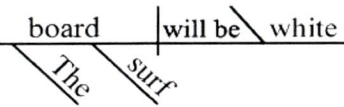

Verb Phrases- Exercise 1
1. The church could be a cathedral.

   church | could be \ cathedral

   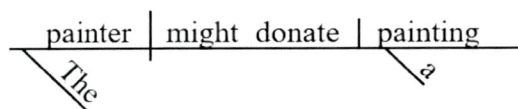

2. James has given money.

   James | has given | money

3. The camp must be fun.

   camp | must be \ fun

4. The surf board will be white.

   board | will be \ white

5. The painter might donate a painting.

   painter | might donate | painting

   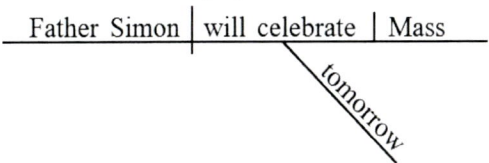

Adverbs- Exercise 1
1. Father Simon will celebrate Mass tomorrow.

   Father Simon | will celebrate | Mass

   tomorrow

2. Modern toasters provide heat rapidly.

   toasters | provide | heat

   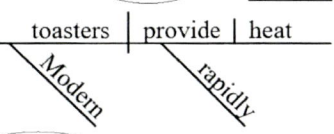

3. Harry stumbled ahead.

   Harry | stumbled

   ahead

4. Virginia's weather can change suddenly.

   weather | can change

   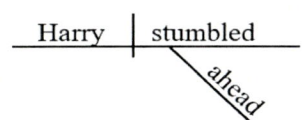

5. We will watch today.

   We | will watch

   today

6. The sun shone brightly.

   sun | shone

   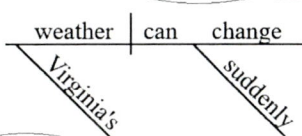

7. The incense floated upward.

   incense | floated

   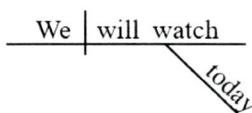

8. Jesus knew the man well.

   Jesus | knew | man

   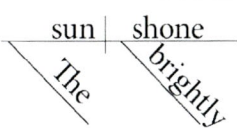

9. Jason reads frequently.

   Jason | reads

   frequently

10. The dangerous blizzard blew snow everywhere.

    blizzard | blew | snow

    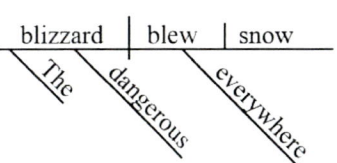

Answer Key **87**

Adverbs-Exercise 3
1. Victoria eagerly bridled her horse.
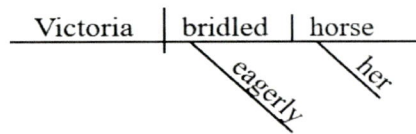

2. The falcon flew below.
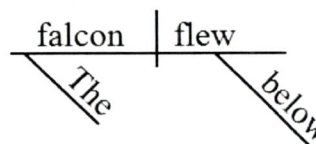

3. The man rudely shouted.
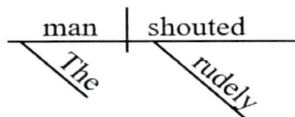

4. Samuel usually prays the Rosary.
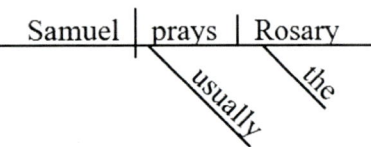

5. The dark clouds quickly approached.
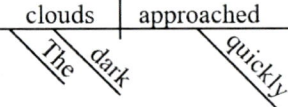

Adverbs- Exercise 4
1.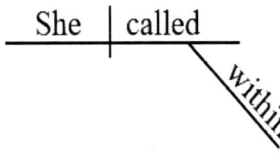

2.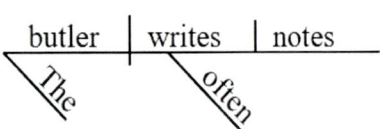

3.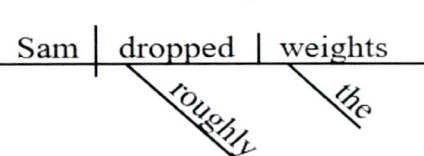

4.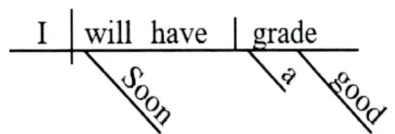

5.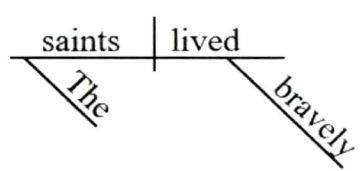

Compound Predicate- Exercise 1
1. Bob knows and loves God.
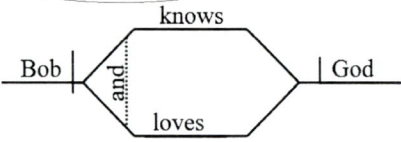

2. Math challenges and improves the mind.
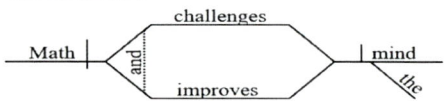

3. Isabelle cooked and baked.
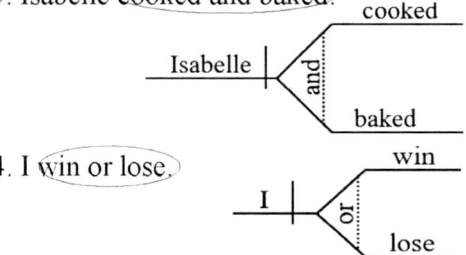

4. I win or lose.

5. St. Thérèse lived and preached a simple life.
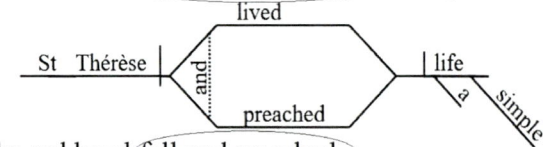

6. The red bowl fell and smashed.
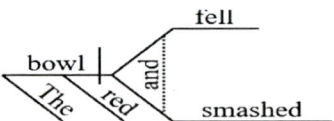

7. Water hydrates and cools.
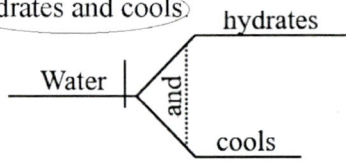

8. Chris lifted and shoved the box.
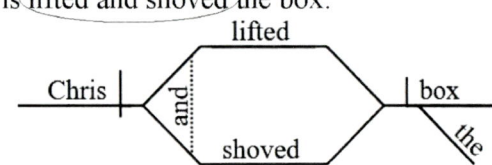

9. Tamara learns and remembers people's names.

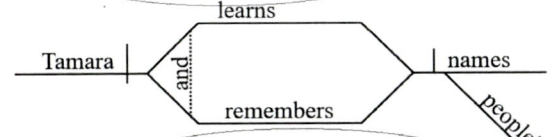

10. A computer hummed and flickered.

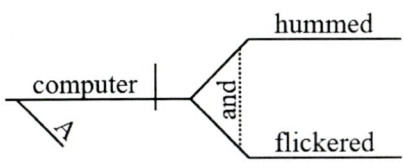

Compound Predicate- Exercise 3
1. Bernadette caught and threw the ball.

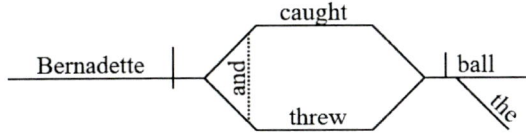

2. The excited athlete sprinted and shouted.

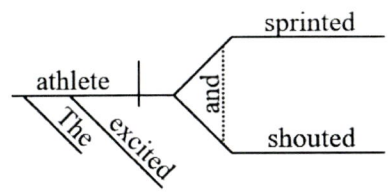

3. The firemen rescued and saved the residents.

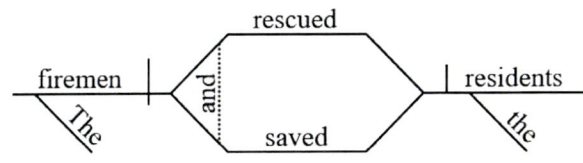

4. The girls danced and jumped. – OR – The girls jumped and danced.

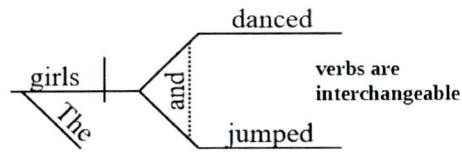

verbs are interchangeable

5. Michael read and absorbed the news.

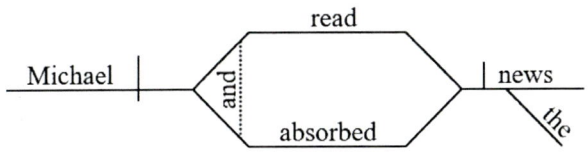

Compound Predicate- Exercise 4
1.

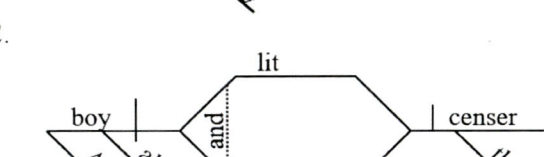

2.

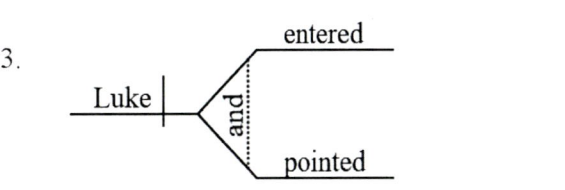

3.

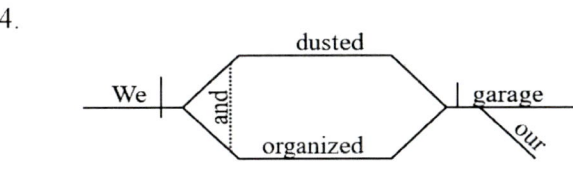

4.

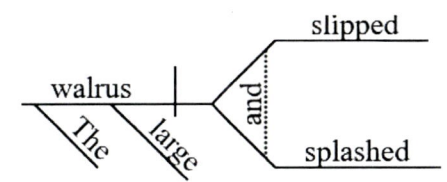

5.

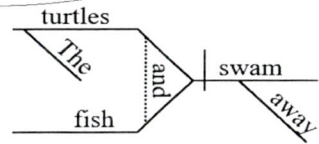

Compound Subject- Exercise 1
1. The turtles and fish swam away.

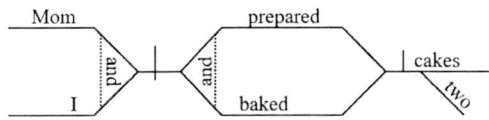

2. Mom and I prepared and baked two cakes.

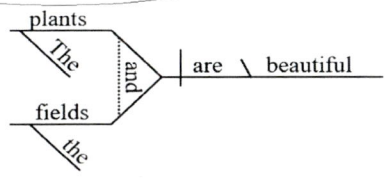

3. The plants and the fields are beautiful.

Answer Key 89

4. Harriet and Thomas slowly walked.
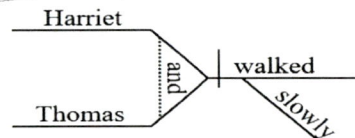

5. A hickory branch and an oak tree fell suddenly.
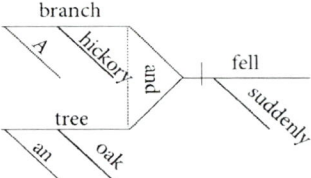

6. Yellow and orange are bright colors.
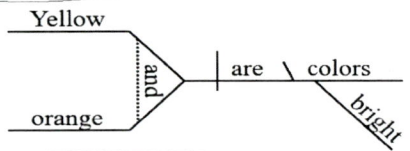

7. The hiking trails and campgrounds are well-kept.
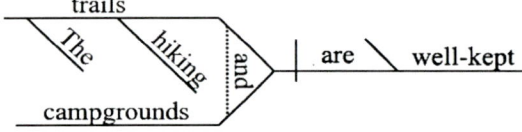

8. Jacinta and her mother sat and talked.
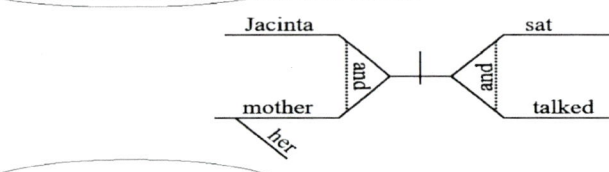

9. Inventors and engineers build future technology.
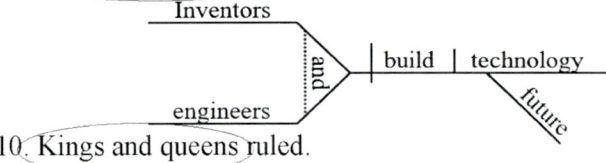

10. Kings and queens ruled.
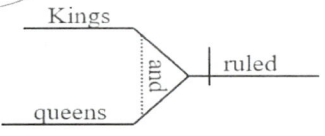

Compound Subject- Exercise 3

1. Joe and the teacher disagreed. – OR – The teacher and Joe disagreed.
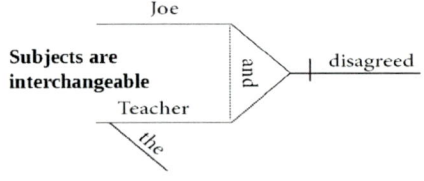

2. The omelets and pancakes cooked. – OR – The pancakes and omelets cooked.
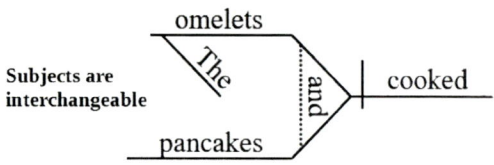

3. Earth and Jupiter are planets. – OR – Jupiter and Earth are planets.
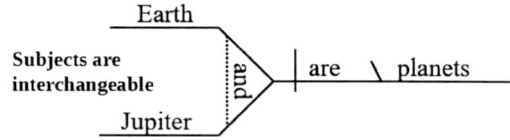

4. The crowd and soccer players watched and listened. – OR – The crowd and soccer players listened and watched.
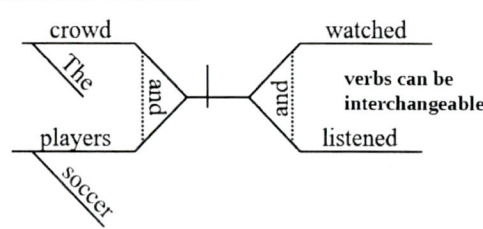

5. Peter and Gulliver discovered and photographed old fossils. – OR – Gulliver and Peter discovered and photographed old fossils.
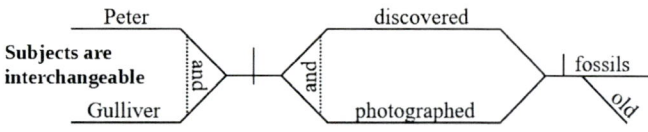

Compound Subject- Exercise 4

1.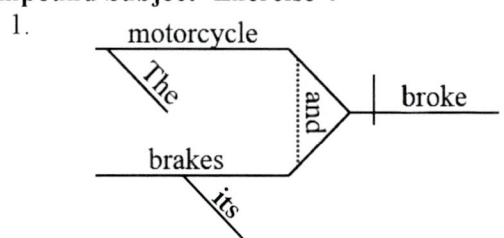

2.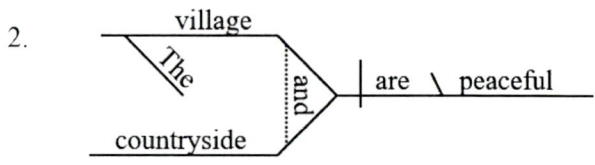

3.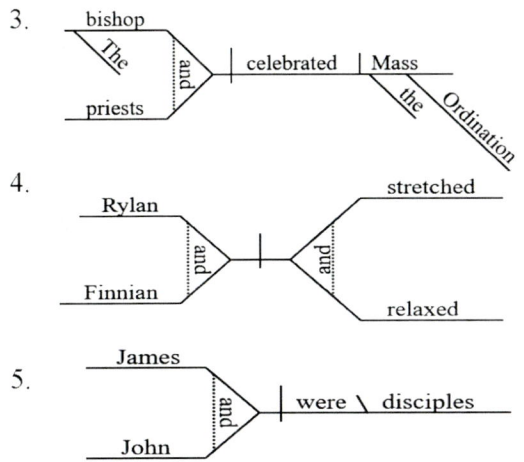

4.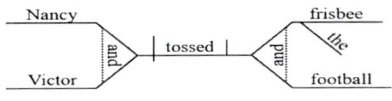

5.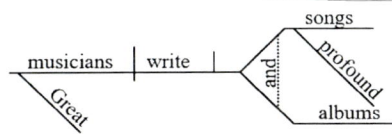

Compound Direct Object- Exercise 1
1. Nancy and Victor tossed the frisbee and football.
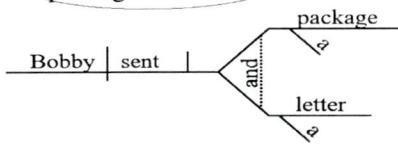

2. Great musicians write profound songs and albums.
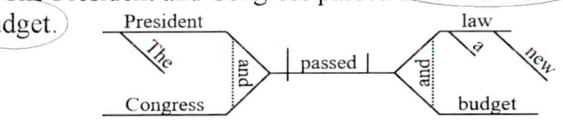

3. Bobby sent a package and a letter.
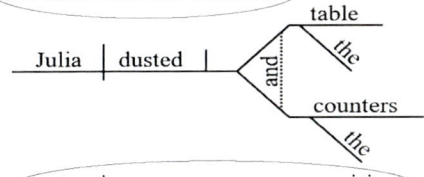

4. The President and Congress passed a new law and budget.
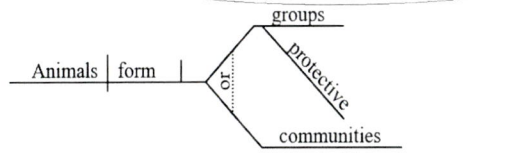

5. Julia dusted the table and the counters.

6. Animals form protective groups or communities.

7. Freddy and Cecelia found and grabbed cups and plates.
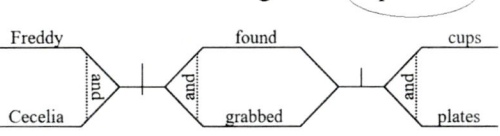

8. The Blessed Virgin brought peace and joy.
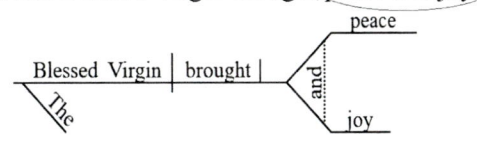

9. The sick boy ate soup and crackers.
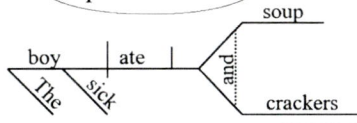

10. The news shocked and angered the parents and the general public.
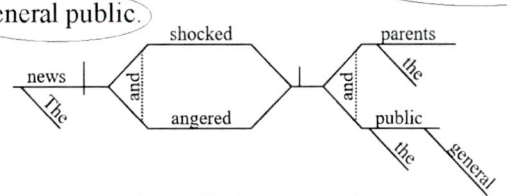

Compound Direct Object-Exercise 3

1. St. John wrote letters and a Gospel.
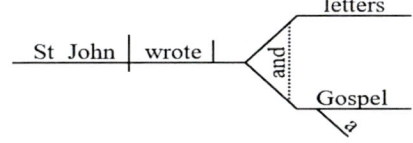

2. Kelly noticed the old couple and the grandchildren.
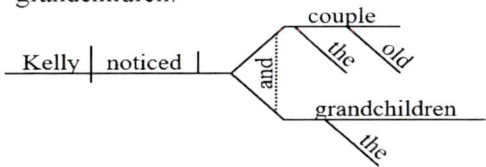

3. Haily washed and dried the bicycle and the helmet. – OR – Haily washed and dried the helmet and the bicycle.
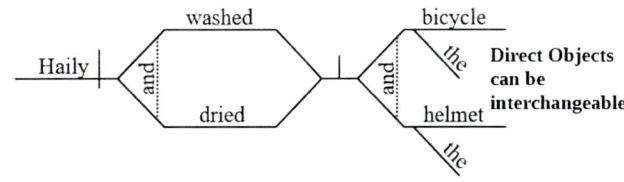

Direct Objects can be interchangeable

Answer Key 91

4. The father saved him and Mary's family.
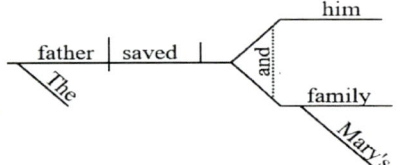

5. Police officers protect citizens and communities. – OR – Police officers protect communities and citizens.
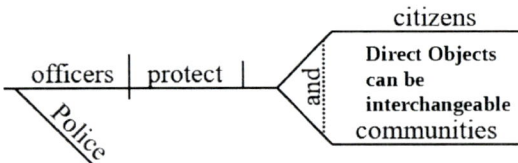

Compound Direct Object Exercise 4
1.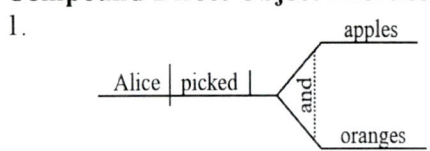
2.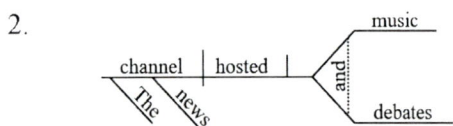
3.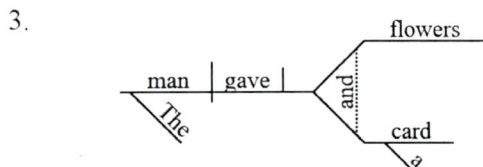
4.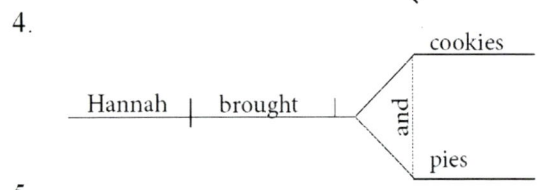
5.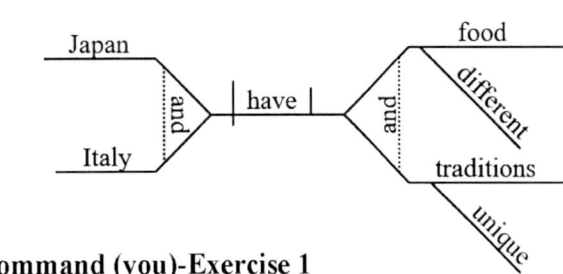

Command (you)-Exercise 1
1. (you) | Stand
2. (you) | Speak
3. (you) | Catch
4. (you) | Come
5. (you) | Jump

Direct Object-Review Exercise 1
1. Christ forgives sins.
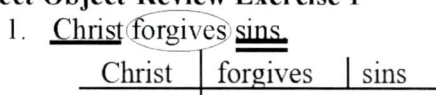
2. The cat bit the toy.
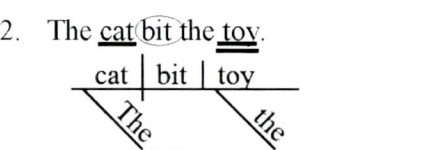
3. Gerald taught the class.
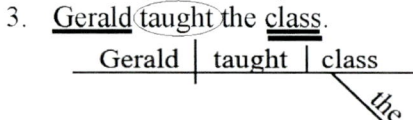
4. The waves smashed the beach.
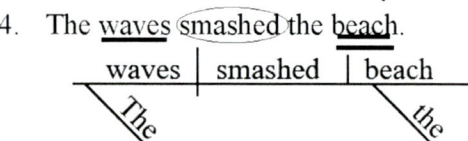
5. The nomad packed a tent.
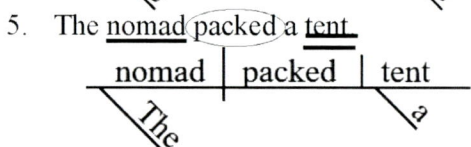

Adjectives- Review Exercise 1
1. This train rumbled.
train | rumbled
2. The older cousin called.
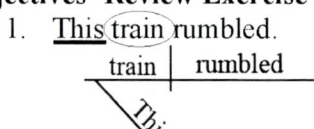
3. Strong storms will arrive.
storms | will arrive
4. He cooks Mexican food.
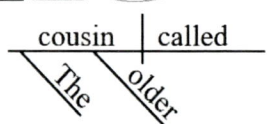
5. Clarissa bought a new dress.
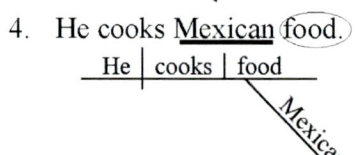

Subjective Complements- Review Exercise 1
1. A ski vacation can be pleasant.

   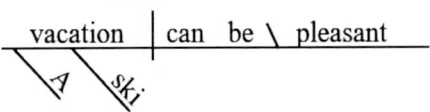

2. Father Michael is a good priest.

   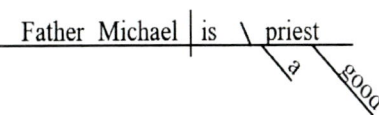

3. Mothers are resilient.

   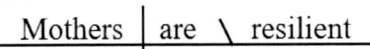

4. The woman will be a nurse.

   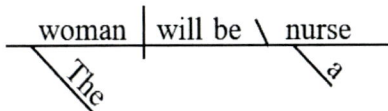

5. This store is huge.

   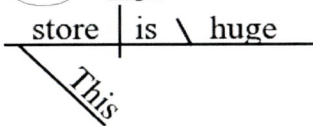

Adverbs (time, place, and manner)- Review Exercise 1
1. Xavier awoke early.

   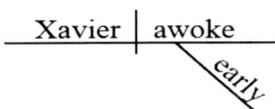

2. The electrician struggled nearby.

   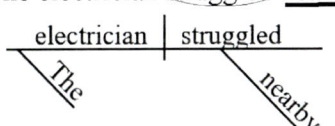

3. Sandra beautifully finished the dress.

   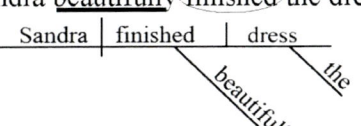

4. Unhappy babies can cry loudly.

   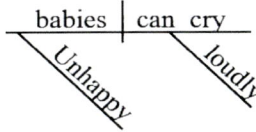

5. He still climbs.

   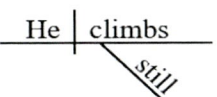

Compound Predicate-Review Exercise 1
1. Matthew reads and writes.

   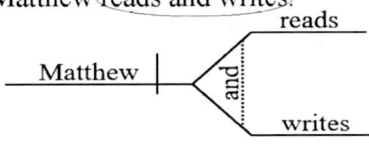

2. The car swerved and braked.

   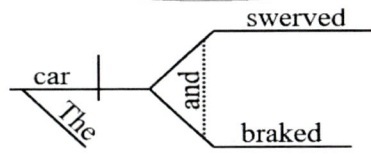

3. Nick proofreads and edits the papers.

   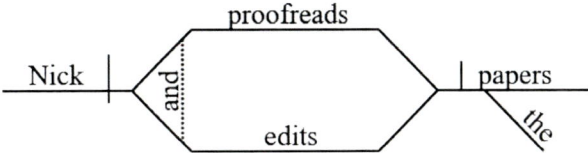

4. A northern wind howled and blew.

   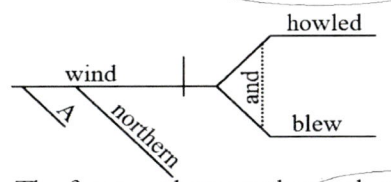

5. The famous photographer took and sent stunning photos.

   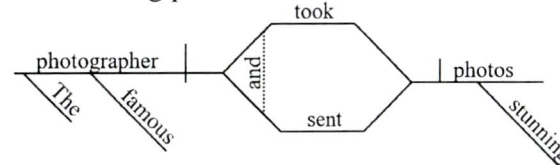

Compound Subject-Review Exercise 1
1. The abbot and the prior received the postulants.

   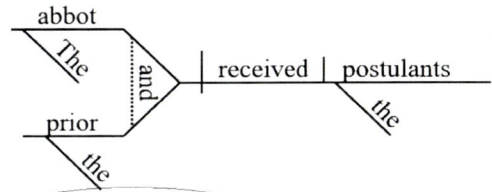

2. Rick and Joanna calculated and determined the budget.

   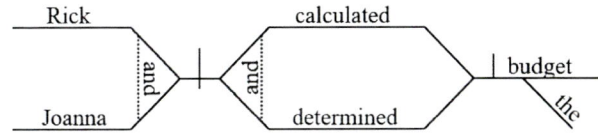

3. Abraham and Sarah soon departed.

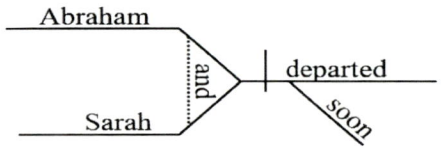

4. My friends and I meet frequently.

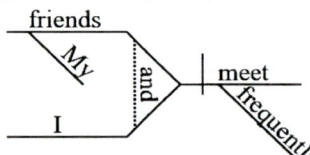

5. Math and science can be difficult subjects.

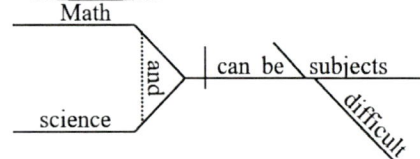

Compound Direct Object-Review Exercise 1

1. My grandfather hopefully will enjoy a vacation and a new car.

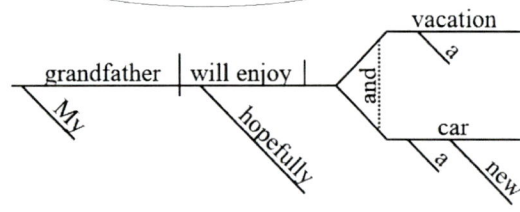

2. The snake crossed the river and the road.

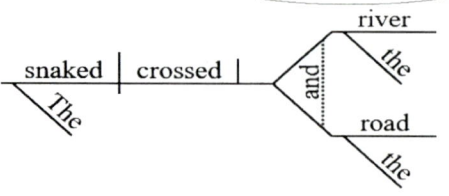

3. Shannon used the brush and the comb.

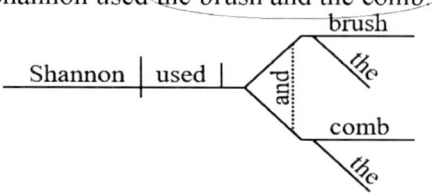

4. Growing towns and cities will create great jobs and communities.

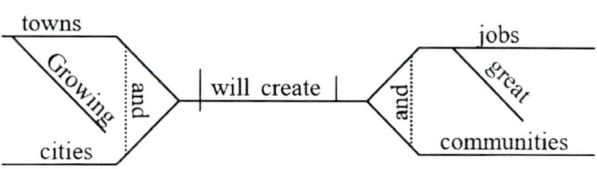

5. Mr. Holmes planted squash and peas.

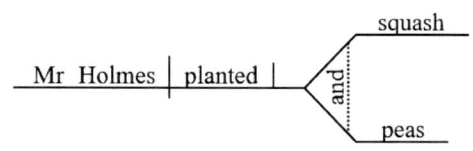